Tokyo Travel Guide 2020 Insiders

Robert Smith

Contenido

Introduction To Japan 5

The History Of Japan 7

Top Tourist Destinations 12

The Japanese Culture 16

Some Things You Should Know Before You Travel To Japan 21

Japanese Food Traditions 26

Tokyo **27**

Mt Fuji 111

Copyright

Copyright © 2020 Robert Smith

All rights reserved. No part of this book may be reproduced in any form or by any electronic or mechanical means including information storage and retrieval systems – except in the case of brief quotations in articles or reviews – without the permission in writing from its publisher, Robert Smith.

All brand names and product names used in this book are trademarks, registered trademarks, or trade names of their respective holders. We are not associated with any product or vendor in this book.

Introduction To Japan

Japan, is a nation where the past meets the future. Also referred to as Nihon or Nippon in Japanese, this island nation is located in East Asia. With a history stretching as far as over 300BC, you can bet that this country has seen it all. Actually, very few nations all over the world have had a colorful history as Japan. Dating back to the prehistoric era and seeing the rise and fall of countless emperors, the rule of the Samurai Warriors and the isolation from the outside world for over 200 years, Japan and the Japanese pride in having a long history that you will definitely enjoy when you hear them. Although Japan was one of the most warlike nations of the early 20th century, this has since changed. Actually, it now serves as a voice of pacifism and restraint at the international stage.

Japan also happens to be one of those countries that has experienced some of the biggest disasters including the World War II atomic bomb, raging fires that have lasted for months, earth quakes and typhoons just to mention a few. The capital of Japan is Tokyo, which boasts of being the world's most populous metropolitan with over 40 million residents!

It's culture stretches back to over a millennia but it is also famous for adopting and creating the latest trends and fashions. If you are educated in the West, Japan can be a difficult country to understand. It can appear full of contradictions. It is dominated by many Japanese corporations but if you read the financial news, it appears as though the country is practically bankrupt. While cities are as high tech and modern as anywhere else, you can still spot tumbledown wooden shacks next to glass fronted designer condominiums.

Amidst modern skyscrapers, you will discover sliding wooden doors leading to traditional chambers with shoji screens, tatami mats and calligraphy, ideal for traditional tea ceremonies. You may find these juxtapositions jarring or perplexing if you are used to the more uniform nature of North American and European cities, but if you clear your mind, start a fresh and acknowledge the layered aesthetics, you will find surprising and interesting places throughout the country.

The West has always identified Japan as a land that combines tradition and modernity, and while many practices and structures are preserved, modern practices and structures will definitely dominate your experience in the country. It was the first country in Asia to independently modernize, and still continues to embrace new aesthetics and technologies. However, unlike in many nations, Japan does seem to have the need to remove or attack older practices, structures, and technologies. New things are basically structured beside old things. This does not necessarily mean that the country embraces massive preservation of historical structures or that the citizens generally practice traditional ceremonies. However, the natives generally believe that if a small portion of the population wants to preserve a building that they own, or to continue on a tradition, they should not be prohibited. As such, development often takes place in a piecemeal fashion, with one building at a time as opposed to large redevelopment projects. You will find that several urban blocks have evolved to align dozens of narrow building that spin 50 or more years of design history.

The History Of Japan

Pre-historic Japan

It is highly likely that Paleolithic people first occupied Japan 35,000 years ago from the Asian mainland. About ten thousand years ago, at the end of the last Ice Age, a culture known as the Jomon was developed (DNA analyses suggest that the Ainu people could be the descendants of the Jomon). The people (Jomon) were hunters, fishermen and gatherers. They also fashioned elaborate clay vessels, wooden houses and fur clothing. In one of the accounts about the third century AD, a queen by the name Himiko is mentioned in a Chinese historical document.

The Yayoi people did the second wave of settlement at around 400 B.C. These introduced weaving, rice cultivation and metalworking. DNA evidence suggests that the origin of these settlers was Korea.

Kofun Period (AD 300-710)

When the 4th century came, the ancestors of the imperial family of the present established the very first unified state in Japan under the Yamato court.

After the Yayoi people followed the Kofun era. The Kofun is the first era of recorded history in the country that was characterized by tumuli, or large burial mounds. The tombs were made for the political class of the era. Within this period, they introduced agricultural tools, weapons and articles from Korea and China. These were led by a class of aristocratic warlords who adopted several Chinese innovations and customs.

Asuka Period (AD 538-710)

It was during the Asuka Period that Buddhism was introduced to Japan (538 to 710), as well as the Chinese writing system. The society was grouped into clans, with the Yamato province as the headquarters.

Nara Period (AD 710-794)

The first stable central government was established between 710 and 794 in Nara. This was a Chinese system of law codes that were referred to as the Ritsuryo system. At this time, Buddhism was the national religion and the people practiced Buddhist architecture and art. It was also during the time when the then government constructed provincial temples referred to as kokubunji. One of the temples constructed during the era was the Todaiji temple, which saw the building of the Great Buddha. At this time, the Chinese practiced calligraphy, and the aristocratic class Buddhism. The agricultural villagers adopted Shintoism.

It was also during the Nara period that the Man'yoshu was developed-this was a collection of the histories of Japan including Kojiki, and Nihon Shoki.

Heian Period (AD 794-1185)

The unique culture of Japan developed quickly between 794 to 1185 during the Heian era. The imperial court turned out enduring prose, poetry and art. The capital moved to what is now Kyoto after which some families started gaining government control to an extent of ruling on behalf of the then emperor. At this time, the existing Chinese-style culture, started being replaced by an indigenous style of culture that was fairly closer to the lives of the people and their surroundings. Additionally, different palaces of the then emperor and various residents of different noble families started incorporating beautiful gardens with different buildings what is referred to as the Shiden-zukuri style of architecture. It was also during the Heian period when some of the literally masterpieces like the Murasaki Shikibu's The Tale of Genji were made.

The Kamakura Period (AD 1185-1333)

In the late Heian period, the Taira family, which was a warrior family that had gained substantial control over the imperial court was overthrown by the Minamoto family after which the Minamoto no Yoritoso was given the coveted title of shogun by the court. The years that followed saw this shogun set up a military style kind of government at Kakakura making it Kamakura shogunate. This ushered a period of military style of leadership. The artists of the time started embracing warrior spirit as well to keep up with the leadership of the time. For instance, statues that were made included those of fierce guardian deities by such sculptures as Unkei and others. Most of these were in the Southern Great Gate of the Tadoiji temple. Literature wasn't left behind; military tales like the tale of Heike were crafted to celebrate the successes of the warriors.

Muromachi Period (AD 1333-1568)

This period was marred with political standoffs between Emperor Go-Daigo and Ashikaga Takauji his former supporter. The emperor had restored some government control to the then imperial court while the Kamakura Shogunate was overthrown by Ashikaga Takauji who then established Muromachi Shogunate. The shogunate had weakened resulting to substantial loss of control over the local warlords. The latter years of this period is what is often referred to as the Sengoku period, which means warring states.

This period also marked the emergence of more plebeian forms of culture since the peasants and the merchants had started to enhance their circumstances. It was also during the period when Chinese-style ink painting started taking root while in theater, the Kyogen and the Noh drama started taking root. Tea ceremonies also increased in popularity during this period and the culture of flower arrangement was born. In terms of Architecture, the Shoin Zukuri style of architecture was born-this had beautiful tatami matted rooms that featured an alcove where different paintings were hung.

The Azuchi-Momoyama Period (1568-1600)

During this period, Toyotomi Hideyoshi and Oda Nobunaga unified the nation-these two were the foremost among the different Sengoku warlords. The period also saw increased contact with Europeans who started influencing art. The people also started embracing a lavish decorateive style in place of Buddhist style-the new style was at its peak in the Osaka Castle, Hideyoshi casle and Nobunaga's Azuchi Castle. The tea ceremony was also officially started by tea master Sen no Rikyo-this was referred to as the Way of Tea.

The Edo Period (AD 1600-1868)

The Tokugawa Shogunate was established in Edo (where Tokyo lies today) after Tokugawa Leyasu defeated the other vassals during the battle of Sekigahara following the death of Toyotomi Hideyoshi. The Tokugawa shoguns then ruled Japan for more than 260 years. During this period, Japan was literally shut off from foreign contact for about 200 years at a time when the shogunate had a policy of national seclusion.

A new culture of down to earth developed at end of the 17th century and at the beginning of the 18th century. This was popular among the townsmen of the older cities of Osaka and Kyoto. It was also during this period when Ihara Saikaku composed the Ukiyo-zoshi (the books of the floating world). There were also the Chikamatsu Monzaemon who portrayed different tragic relationships between women and men through puppet plays.

The printing of books started taking root in the shogun capital of Edo (now Tokyo). Woodblock print (Ukiyoe) was also established, which saw the production of portraits of different actors.

The Meiji Period (1868-1912)

It was during the Meiji restoration when the political authority was restored back to the imperial court from the shogunate. The national seclusion policy also ended and a new culture and civilization (Western culture) started taking root. There was also the birth of the modern Japanese literature including Futabatei Shimei's novel known as Ukigumo, which means Drifting Clouds.

The other periods were the Taisho Period (1912-1926), the Showa period (1926-1989) and the modern period. All these are a story of how Japan has grown from the prehistoric country to a modern city that boasts of being one of those countries that has risen from the ashes.

Top Tourist Destinations

Japan is one of the most celebrated tourist destinations in the world. As said earlier, it is a blend of modern and traditional, with several ancient buildings and temples coexisting with modern achievements in technology and architecture. While touring the county, you may be mesmerized by the Japanese culture and history in one day, and then get mind blown by their technological developments on the next day. Nearly all historical sites still retain their original purpose, while remaining open to the public at the same time. You can see the natural beauty of the country all year.

Note: Japan has one of the lowest crime rates in the world, which makes it suitable for travelers. Here is an overview of the top tourist destinations in the country:

***Hiroshima peace memorial**

This is a haunting tribute established to pay tribute to the lives that were lost when Hiroshima was hit by an atomic bomb on August 6, 1945. It is set in a park with only one building known as Genbaku Dome that was left standing in the area after the bomb was dropped. It is a harsh reminder of a world at war that serves as an aide memoir of the importance of human life. It also honors the victims so that they are never forgotten.

***Kiyomizu-dera**

This is Buddhist temple located in Eastern Kyoto, and whose origins can be traced back to 798. The temple is kept in harmony with nature by an indoor waterfall that stretches from the outside river, and not a single nail was used in construction. Locals used to jump off the edge of the fall to have a wish granted, but you can enjoy the shrines, artwork, and talismans on display without having to risk your life and limb.

*Jigokudani Monkey Park

This is a hot spring area located near Nagano. The name means Jigokudani, and is as a result of boiling water and steam that bubbles out of the frozen ground, surrounded by formidably cold forests and steep cliffs. It is famous for the large numbers of Snow Monkeys that migrate to the valley in winter when the park is covered in snow. The monkeys descend from the forest and steep cliffs to sit in the hot and warm springs, and then return to the forests in the evenings.

*Himeji castle

This is considered the best remaining example of the Japanese castle architecture. The castle was fortified during the feudal period to help defend against enemies, but it has been renovated several times throughout history and mirrors the different design periods. It miraculously survived the World War II bombings, and is often seen in foreign and domestic films. The white design and exterior gives the castle an illusion of a bird taking off, which is probably why it was nicknamed, "white egret castle".

*Great Buddha of Kamakura

This is a colossal outdoor representation of one of the most celebrated Buddhist figures in Japan known as Amida Buddha. It is cast in bronze, and is over 13 meters tall, weighing almost 93 tons. It is reported to date back to 1252. While it was originally placed in a small wooden temple, it now stands in the open air since the original temple was drained in a tsunami in the fifteenth century.

*Todaiji temple

This temple is located in Nara, and is a feat of engineering. Not only is it the largest wooden building in the world, it is also home to the largest bronze Buddha statue in the world. It is surrounded by wildlife and gardens, and at the center lies the Kegon school of Buddhism. The grounds hold several Buddhist and Japanese artifacts throughout history. You will find deer roaming freely as messengers of the Shinto gods on the ground.

*Tokyo Tower

The Tokyo Tower is a manifestation of modern life and the advancement in technology. It was inspired by the Eiffel tower design, and is the second tallest man made structure in the country. It also serves as an observation and communications tower. While there, you can climb the tower for incomparable views of Tokyo city, the surrounding areas, as well as the restaurants and shops around.

*Tokyo imperial palace

The Tokyo Imperial Palace is home to the Emperor of Japan. It also serves as an administration center, as well as a museum to display Japanese history and art. The palace is based on the ruins of older castles that were destroyed by either war or fire. Architects have also honored the past by including design elements of the various eras in the palace. There are traditional Japanese gardens all round the modern palace with several functions and reception rooms to welcome the public and receive guests.

*Mount Fuji

Standing at 3,776 meters, Mount Fuji is the tallest mountain in Japan. The exceptional symmetrical cone of the volcano is a popular symbol of the country, and it is often depicted in photographs and art. It is also a popular tourist attraction for climbers and sightseers. It can take between 3 and 8 hours to climb the mountain, and two to five to climb down.

*Golden Pavilion

The Temple of the Golden Pavilion, also known as Kinkaku-ji, is the most popular tourist attraction in Kyoto and Japan. Initially, it was built as a retirement home for Shogun Ashikaga Yoshimitsu back in the 14th century. Sadly, the pavilion was burned down by a young monk in 1950 who had become obsessed with it. The temple was rebuilt five years later as an exact replica of the original. The main emphasis is on the building, as well as the surrounding gardens being in harmony with each other. It is covered in gold leaf that illuminates its reflection in the pond and the reflection of the pond on the building.

The Japanese Culture

Throughout history, Japan has absorbed several ideas from other countries, including forms of cultural ‚expression, customs, and technology. It has also developed its own unique culture while incorporating these adaptations. Today, the Japanese lifestyle is a rich combination of Western influenced modern culture, as well as Asian influenced traditional culture.

Traditional culture

Some of the traditional performing arts that are still highly active in Japan include bunraku, kyogen, noh and kabuki.

Kabuki is a sort of classical theater that developed in the early 17th century. It features the rhythm of the lines spoken by the actors, flamboyant makeup, extravagant costumes, and the use of mechanical devices to produce special effects on stage. Generally, the makeup reflects the moods and personalities of the characters. Majority of the plays draw on Edo or medieval period themes, and all the actors are men, including those that play female roles.

Noh, on the other hand, is the oldest form of musical theater in Japan. The story is told both through dialogue, as well as through utai (basically singing), mai (daning), and hayashi (ideally, musical accompaniment). In addition, the main actor, usually dressed in an embroidered silk costume bright in color and wearing a lacquered wooden mask. The mask may depict characters such as an old man, a young body, a ghost, a divine figure, and a young or old woman.

Kyogen is a kind of classical comic theater performed with highly stylized lines and actions. It is usually performed in between noh performances, but it is mostly performed on its own right sometimes.

Bunraku is a type of Puppet Theater that was popularized around the end of the 16th century. It is performed as an accompaniment of narrative music and singing played on the shamisen, a 3 stringed instrument. It is widely known as one of the most refined types of Puppet Theater in the world.

Other traditional arts, like the *ikebana and the tea ceremony*, still thrive as part of the daily lives of the Japanese people. The Sado orchado, or tea ceremony, is a highly structured technique of preparing green tea. However, there is so much more to the ritual than just making and serving green tea. It is a deep, complete art that requires a delicate sensitivity and a wide range of knowledge. The technique also encourages an appreciation of nature, and explores the purpose of life.

The Ikebana, or the Japanese flower arrangement, evolved over seven centuries ago in Japan, and is believed to have originated from the early Buddhist flower offerings. It is generally differentiated from completely decorative use of flowers from the extreme care taken in choosing all the elements of each work, including the container, the plant material, how the branches relate to the surrounding space and the container, as well as where each flower and branch is placed.

Modern Culture

Classical music originated from the West to Japan, and enjoys a broad following. There are concerts held all over the country. The country has also produced several conductors, violinists, and pianists that perform all over the world. Ever since Kurosawa Akira bagged the Golden Lion Award in 1951 at the Venice Film Festival, Japanese cinema has been the center of global attention. Works by great directors such as Ozu Yasujiro and Mizoguchi Kenji have also been widely hailed. Kitano Takeshi recently won the Golden Lion Award at the Venice Film Festival in 1997 with HANA-BI.

Modern Japan is a highly urbanized society. Its cities have a long history, starting with the first imperial capitals, such as Kyoto and Nara. These cities were designed after Ch'ang-an, a Chinese T'ang dynasty, and were a reflection of the architectural principles of the Chinese imperial court. A checkerboard of grid streets was enclosed by walls and gates that revolved around the institutions of imperial power. They focused mainly on an imperial compound. During the civil wars of the 15th and 16th centuries, the typical urban place was the castle town, a structured city that functioned as the headquarters for the provincial warlord. The castle towns were still the main regional economic and administrative centers all over the Tokugawa period. They were segregated spatially along class lines, and their social organization and spatial layout put emphasis on the domestic convenience and defensive needs of the lord, as well as his retinue.

After the restoration of the Meiji, most castle towns diminished as migration to new centers of economic and industrial opportunity led to a renovation of the urban network. Enclaves of Asian and Western traders formed lucrative cosmopolitan communities in many treaty ports. Industrialization was centered on established cities such as Osaka and Tokyo, as well as cities and towns that thrived in textiles, shipbuilding and mining. The corridor that aligned the Pacific seaboard between Osaka and Tokyo slowly developed as the central axis of the industrial complex. During the World War II, nearly all the cities were severely damaged, but were quickly rebuilt after the war. A large-scale urban migration also took place throughout the fifty's and sixty's due to the massive economic development and industrialization. By the sixty's, urban sprawl had led to enormous megalopolises.

Approximately a quarter of the population resides in the greater Tokyo region and about less than ten percent of the population lives in the rural areas. The concentration of heavy industrial facilities during the fifty's and sixty's in densely populated areas led to environmental pollution on an extraordinary scale. Quality of life issues, such as environmental pollution, population density, as well as the quality of the household stock, is still a problem. The existence of the earliest forms of architecture are mirrored in the austere simplicity of a few Shinto shrines. The style is believed to reflect prehistoric influences from Austronesia and Oceania. It features steeply pitched roofs that have deep overhanging eaves, as well as floors raised from the ground.

Chinese architectural styles were incorporated in the sixth century, especially for the imperial structures and the Buddhist temples. The style of construction of these buildings went a long way towards resisting earthquakes.

A distinctly Japanese architectural style evolved during the period of the aristocratic Heian. It featured the use of covered walkways and verandas to link rooms, the use of folding and sliding screens to partition larger spaces, and the use of thick straw mats on the floors. Majority of the elements of this style were incorporated to the more ordinary living circumstances. By the time of the Tokugawa period, the wealth merchant and samurai homes included several of these elements. Housing has been built following Western lines since World War II.

While most homes still have traditional elements, most of the living space is designed with generically modern furnishings. Condominiums and contemporary apartments are even less likely to have Japanese style rooms that the single-family dwellings.

Generally, contemporary cultural attitudes towards and utilization of space depends on clear distinctions between the private and public spaces, defined along the dimensions of smell, touch, sound and sight. Bodies are pressed together in crowded public spaces without comment. However, in most private sittings, it would be preposterous to even touch a stranger. In the private settings that are occupied and used by a group of people on a progressive basis, clear spatial patterns mirror the internal hierarchies of the social position within the group, as well as between the group, and the others.

Some Things You Should Know Before You Travel To Japan

Respect, addressing someone

For Japanese people, bowing is nothing less than a form of art, respect pounded into the heads of the children from the moment they enter school. For tourists, an attempt of a bow at the waist, or a simple inclination of the head will suffice. The level of inclination and the duration will depend on the person you are addressing. A friend, for instance, may get a lightning fast thirty degree bow, while an office superior might receive a slow and extended seventy degree bow. It is all about circumstance and position.

Apart from bowing, addressing a person in the right manner is equally important. It's just the same as a certain "Dr. James" would feel slightly insulted if you were to refer to him as simply "James", and similarly would a Japanese if you failed to include the suffix "san" after their last name, or if you are trying to be specially respectful, "sama". Children are usually content with just using their first names, but if you like, you could add the suffix "kun" for boys and "chan for girls.

Table manners

If you are at a dinner party and happen to receive drinks, do not rush to raise the glass to your lips. Everyone is bound to be served, and someone will take the lead, present a speech, raise his drink, and then exclaim "kampai!" which essentially means cheers.

Most Japanese restaurants will normally give you a small wet cloth. Use this to wash your hands before you eat, then fold it carefully and set it aside on the table. Do not touch it on any part of your face or use it as a napkin.

It is OK to make loud noises and slurp noodles while eating. Surprisingly, slurping hot foods, such as ramen is considered polite to show that you are enjoying it. You are also allowed to raise the bowl to your mouth when using chopsticks to eat, in order to make it easier to feed, especially bowls of rice.

Right before you dig in, whether it is a sample at a supermarket or a seven course dinner, it is considered polite to say" itadakimasu", which simply means "I will receive."

*No tipping

You are not allowed to tip in any situation in Japan, including personal care, restaurants and cabs. In fact, it is considered slightly insulting to tip someone. The price you have given has covered the services you have asked for, so why pay more?

In case you find yourself in a large area such as Tokyo, and you cannot speak any Japanese, a waitress or waiter may take the extra money you happen to leave in order to avoid dealing with the awkward situation of having to explain the concept that there is no tipping in broken English. Just keep in mind that a price is a price.

Chopsticks

Depending on the restaurant you decide to go to on an evening, you might be required to use chopsticks. If you are not adept with using chopsticks for some reason, try to learn before you pass through the immigration. In case you happen to dine with a Japanese, do not be surprised by their amazement at your ability to use chopsticks like a Japanese.

Thresholds

Be sure to take off your shoes at the entrance to most hotels and businesses, and all homes. A rack will usually be provided to place your shoes, and you will be assigned a pair of guest slippers. However, many Japanese carry a pair of indoor slippers just in case. Avoid using slippers when stepping onto a tatamimat (used in many Japanese hotels and homes), and be cautious to remove the toilet slippers placed for you in the bathroom. For instance, it is extremely bad to enter the main room of a house again while wearing the same slippers you were using across dirty linoleum.

Masks

Sterilized masks, such as those you would see in an emergency room, are popularly used by municipal workers, office ladies and salary men to prevent other people from contracting their germs. When you think about it, it is rather sensible, considering the fact that masks do not really protect the wearer so much as those around him. It could be for fear of spreading a simple cold, or about exposing other people. Nevertheless, do not let it concern you on your vacation.

Conformity

Groups of Japanese students were asked to identify the risks facing children today, and the majority of them agreed on one thing: individualism. The society in Japan is focused on the group, while western cultures are centered on the individual. So, does this mean that the Japanese people are merely worker bees in a vast hive of concrete and steel? Of course not, but their exhibition of such individual characteristics are calculated carefully and provided in doses. It is not acceptable to draw attention to yourself as an individual. Do not talk on the phone in crowded public areas such as buses or trains, avoid eating as much as possible while on the go, and do not blow your nose in public. The main problem with this is that foreigners cannot avoid simply standing out. You will stick out like aching thumbs despite the number of times you have been there, or how much you know about their culture and society.

For this reason, being in Japan tends to give foreigners rank of D-level celebrities. You will get shouts for attention, glances, calls to have pictures taken with the locals, and even requests for autographs.

Bathing

There are active and lively bathhouses in Japan. You can find neighborhood bathhouses, or Sento, from a small town on the island of Shikoku to the largest location in Shinjuku. Hot springs, or Onsen, are extremely popular as weekend expedition resorts. However, unlike in the western cultures, you are supposed to bath after you have washed and rinsed, and just feel like soaking in hot water for ten to thirty minutes. To be sure, it is an acquired taste, but it can be very relaxing. In case you are invited in a Japanese household, the honor of having the bath first will be given to you, normally before dinner. Be sure not to make the water dirty in any way. The sacredness of the bath, or ofuro, is of utmost importance. If you have the chance, find some time to take a visit a sento. These are places with no barriers, with no regard for language, age, or skin color; well, they are divided by sex, except for a few mixed bathing areas.

Speaking English

Until you prove otherwise, the Japanese people will generally assume that you are a native speaker. Even during a short visit, you will spot:

*A random person walking up to you and asking where you are from. Well, this may seem friendly at first. But it is easy to see how the constant celebrity status can be frustrating or confusing for travelers who do not speak English. Although you may speak a little or fluent Japanese, the preferred default language is English. Most Japanese will insist on using their own ability to speak English to converse to foreigners however limited despite the fact that the other person may have more knowledge of the local tongue.

Safety

Japan is a very safe country. Nonetheless, it is generally advisable to be safe in your travels and take care of your belongings. Here are some things you should be aware of:

*The fear of crime is very high in Japan, especially among the Japanese citizens.

*Murders take place. People are attacked, swindled, beaten, raped, assaulted, and robbed.

However, the low crime rate in Japan is evident when you spot businessmen sleeping on a park bench after missing the last train.

Japanese Food Traditions

The two main staples of the Japanese diet are noodles and rice. Rice is served at every meal, either steamed or boiled. There are many varieties of noodles. The most popular include soba (brown threadlike noodles made from buckwheat flour), ramen (thin and curly noodles, made from wheat flour), and udon (thick and white noodles also made from wheat flour). Some of the other staples are soy sauce and various other soybean products. They include fermented soybean paste known as miso, and tofu.

Other common ingredients in the Japanese food include sesame seed products, seaweed, ginger, daikon, and bamboo shoots. Japanese pickles known as tsukemono are included in every meal. Seafood is also abundant in this island nation.

Their natural beverage is green tea, although you can also find black tea. Sake and beer are also very popular.

Sushi (basically rice with fresh raw seafood), and sashimi (soy sauce with fresh raw seafood) are two specially Japanese foods. Both rely on freshly caught seafood or fish. Dish made in a single pot are popular throughout the country.

Sukiyaki is a dish prepared using paper thin slices of beef, vegetables, and tofu cubed cooked in broth. Basically, shabu-shabu is simply vegetables and beef, also prepared in broth and then dipped in flavorful sauces. Different regions have their own selections of their preferred foods.

Residents of the cold northern island of Hokkaido enjoy barbecued meats, corn and potatoes. Western Japan foods are usually more delicately flavored when compared to those in the east.

The Japanese are famous for using very fresh ingredients when cooking. They are fond of using fresh and seasonal foods for their meals. They buy it the same day that it is cooked. They are also known for their ability to arrange food in such a way that it looks beautiful. It is no wonder that the Japanese have relatively longer life spans, as well as a low rate of heart disease.

Mealtime customs

The Japanese generally have three main meals per day, with the main ingredient being rice, or noodles sometimes. Pickles and Miso soup are also served as well. The simplest meals are the ones eaten early in the day. A typical breakfast is made of miso soup, rice and a side dish, such as grilled fish or an egg. You will also find that the Japanese people love to eat noodles a lot for lunch, as well as a snack. A take out or restaurant stand known as a noodle house is also a popular spot for lunch.

Lunch is characterized by a bowl of broth with fish, seaweed, and vegetables. A traditional box lunch known as the bento is packed into a small and flat box with dividers. It is packed with small portions of vegetables, fish, meat, and rice. Readymade bento is sold at stores for takeout, and there are even Western style ingredients such as sausages and spaghetti in some.

Young locals are fond of stuffed rice balls known as onigiri. Many Japanese people have turned to Western style food for both lunch and breakfast, particularly in the cities. But most people still prefer to eat traditional dinners, such as fish, pickles, soup and rice. Seasonal fresh fruit make for a great dessert. In the afternoon, the locals prefer to take sweets with green tea. You are basically supposed to grasp food with chopsticks and then lift it to your mouth. You should never stick the chopsticks into a piece of food, or use them to pass food back and forth. As said earlier, it is permitted to sip soup directly from the bowl. On the other hand, people at a Japanese meal tend to fill one another's drinking glasses, as opposed to their own. In addition, they do not eat while doing other things, like driving or walking. A Japanese car company once stated that some of its seatbelts in the United States had malfunctioned because the Americans spilled too much food in the cars!

Shibuya

First of all, where is Shibuya?

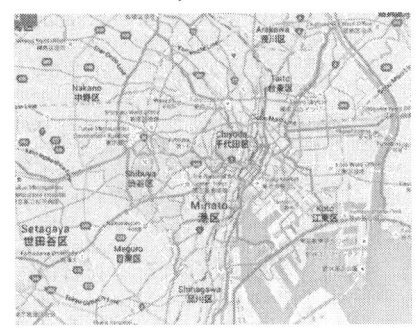

Geographically speaking, it occupies the southwest side of central Tokyo (see the red area in the left image). It can be found on the famous Yamanote Line, which is a train rail that goes around and around on the perimeter of Chiyoda Ward, where the Imperial Palace and its gigantic gardens lie. In fact, Yamanote Line is also where the tired businessmen occasionally take their late night naps, so that after a few rounds they can go back to work without the need to visit home at all. Just to give you a vague idea about the extremely high number of train and metro lines that enmesh the metropolis, here is a list of the ones going through Shibuya, which is a popular destination for both tourists and locals (Note: you can also find the whole metro/train map of Tokyo at the end of the book). Metro: Ginza Line, Hanzomon Line, Fukutoshin Line; train: JR Yamanote Line, JR Chuo Line, JR Saikyo Line, Keio Inokashira Line, Tokyu Toyoko Line, Tokyu Denentoshi Line, Tokyu Setagaya Line. And of course there are many more that pass very close to central Shibuya.

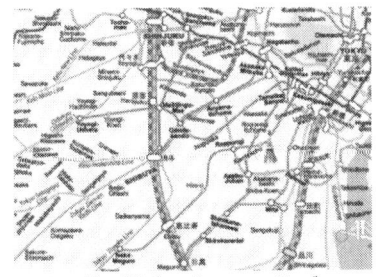

Credit: Google Maps

Credit: flickr, Damon Taylor

What should you know about Shibuya?

According to one of the theories, this area used to be an inlet and was called the "Village of Salt Valley" (Shioya no Sato). This "Shioya" later changed to "Shibuya", and has stuck until this day. One would have to go back all the way to the prehistoric ages to find the first known dwellers. Much later during the Muromachi Period (1336-1573), a village began to form on this land, which kept developing until the establishment of Tokyo in 1868. And finally in 1932 after countless merges and separations, the current borders were drawn (compare the two images below; the left image shows

Credit: Wikipedia   Credit: Wikipedia

Shibuya in 1952, the right one nowadays).
What else?
Its current population is about 200 thousand people, however during daytime this number increases to 540 (!) thousand. Most of the citizens are living alone, unmarried and renting an apartment, as opposed to buying one. Many of them seem to leave after a while, but as there are new ones moving in right away, the actual population of the ward does not change that much. It is a place, where everyone would love to live at least once in a lifetime, before they settle down somewhere else. Approximately 350 thousand people come here to work everyday. And there are over 32 thousand offices (27% of these are in the retail industry) to employ them. Shibuya is one of the most popular and easily accessible places to work. Central Shibuya has been evolving at an incredible speed. A project to completely re-develop the Shibuya Station and its vicinity has begun and Shibuya Hikarie, a cultural and business center, was first completed in 2012 as part of this project. In July 2014, the construction of the station's East Tower began. It is expected to be complete by 2020, and this will make Shibuya Station the tallest station in all of Japan with its planned 270 meters. By 2027, work on the West Tower and the Central Tower will be also finished. Moreover, they are planning a big bus terminal near the towers, which will connect directly to the airport (to be completed in 2018). Finally, in the southern part of this area,

Shibuya River will emerge once again, surrounded by a relaxing park.

What can be found near the station, besides the thousands of workplaces and six universities (there are 138 universities and colleges in the 23 Special Wards alone, which is at least twice as many as in Boston, London or Beijing), that make so many tourists and locals want to visit or live here? The answer is social/night life and entertainment. Everyday, hundreds and hundreds of people wait for their friends or co-workers near the Hachiko Statue in front of the northern Hachiko Gate of the station. This statue was created in memory of a dog, Hachiko, who, even after his owner had passed away, kept waiting for him everyday for 9-10 years at the Shibuya Station. The owner was a professor at the Agricultural Department of the Former Imperial University of Tokyo, named Ueno Hidesaburo, who suddenly died in 1925. 80 years have passed since the death of Hachiko, and the current staff of the Agricultural Department has decided to build a new statue with both the professor and his dog standing together. The first Hachiko statue was erected in Shibuya in 1934, however it was removed during World War II in the name of metal contribution, only to be reinstalled in 1948 after the war was over.

Credit: Photozou, B4 たかし

Another favorite spot to meet is at the Moyai Statue, near the Western Gate of the station. It was a present by Nii-jima (a volcanic island in the Philippine Sea) in 1980, celebrating the 100th anniversary of their administration being transferred to the Tokyo Government.

Credit: flickr, Toshihiro Gamo

After meeting up with someone in front of the Hachiko Statue, you must first follow the crowd to the famous crossing, where roughly 3,000 people cross at each green light.

Credit: flickr, Kojach

Once you have sort of bobbed to the other side of the street in a wave of people, looking around, you may come realize that it will not be easy to choose where to eat or drink: within the vicinity of the main station, there are currently 621 bars, 563 Japanese restaurants, 337 cafes, 99 ramen restaurants, and 64 sushi restaurants, just to mention a few categories.

The most popular izakayas (Japanese style pubs) are:

Watami
Address: Dogenzaka Center Bldg. 5F, Dogenzaka 2-29-8, Shibuya-ku, Tokyo
Phone: +81-3-5456-6028
Hours: 17:00-3:00 (Mon. – Thu. and Sun.), 17:00-5:00 (Fri. – Sat., and the day before any national holiday)

Doma-Doma
Address: Kaleido Shibuya Miyamasuzaka 6F, Shibuya 1-12-1, Shibuya-ku, Tokyo
Phone: +81-50-5786-5855
Hours: 17:00-5:00 (weekdays), 16:00-5:00 (weekends)

For something more special, for example a date, *SKY BAR* is recommended, where you can gaze at the illuminated city at night from a 9th floor lounge.

SKY BAR
Address: Nagashima Daiichi Bldg. 9F, Dogenzaka 1-22-12, Shibuya-ku, Tokyo
Phone: +81-50-5786-1976

Hours: 18:00-5:00 (Mon. – Sun. and the day before any national holiday), 18:00-4:00 (national holidays)

If it is sushi that you are looking for, at *Zauo* you can catch your own fish, which, once you actually succeed in doing so, the staff will prepare for you to eat:

Zauo
Address: Hymanten Jinnan Bldg. B1, Jinnan 1-19-3, Shibuya-ku, Tokyo
Phone: +81-50-5786-4190
Hours: 17:00-23:00 (weekdays), 11:30-23:00 (weekends and national holidays)

There is of course a much more relaxed way to eat sushi, especially if the food is carried to your table on conveyer belts:

Mawashizushi Katsu
Address: A-Bldg. 8F Food Mall Dining Plaza, Udagawa-cho 21-1, Shibuya-ku, Tokyo
Phone: +81-3-5728-4282
Hours: 11:00-22:00, closed on Sundays

And, in case the occasion demands a rather formal setting, you are sure to impress your guests at:

Seiryu Hatsu-tsubomi
Address: Shibuya Square Bldg. A-Wing B1, Dogenzaka 1-9-5, Shibuya-ku, Tokyo
Phone: +81-50-5518-7122
Hours: 17:00-23:00 (Mon. – Sat.), 17:00-22:30 (Sun. and national holidays)

After eating and drinking, you will still need to choose from among 24 different karaoke places. The most popular ones are *Big Echo*, *Utahiroba* and *Karaoke-kan*, as they tend to have the biggest selection of songs and their prices are affordable (especially the last two). Also, if you are into shopping, there are 215 retail stores on the Dogenzaka Street alone, which is the main street of Shibuya Center-Gai.

A brief history of Center-Gai

The first constructions started along the shore of the local Uda River in 1929, where restaurants and cafes began to pop up after 1935. Unfortunately, the river used to flood after every heavy rain, causing trouble for these establishments. Right before the 1964 Tokyo Olympics, Uda River became an underdrain to allow for more surface area to build on. In 1973, Center-Gai reached its current form, with the famous arch (see the photo above). This area was (unfortunately) renamed in 2011 as "Basketball Street" in order to change the image of the street, to a more international, healthy and energetic one. The fact that the biggest basketball store in Japan is actually on this very street (*GALLERY 2*) has apparently also aided in their decision. One of the main symbols of Center-Gai has been *Shibuya 109*, a large shopping mall with many female apparel stores inside. It was built by Tokyu Group, which owns many train lines within Tokyo, and the name came from a play on words: 109 can be read as "to" (ten) and "kyu" (nine) in Japanese. On a weekend or a holiday, it has an average of 35 thousand visitors, from which we can already assume the great influence it has been having on the contemporary clothing trends among women and teenage girls. Besides their clothing chains within Japan, they also opened their first store in Hong Kong in 2015.

Credit: Wikimedia, DeepSkyBlue

Credit: Wikimedia, Aimaimyi

Proceeding east from the station, you could visit one of the best cigar bars in Tokyo: *Sol Cubano*. It is on the Meiji-dori, just across the Shibuya Police Station. They have all kinds of Cuban cigars, which you can enjoy with a Cuban or a South-American rum and smooth chocolate.

Sol Cubano
Address: Sato Estate Bldg. New Bldg. 3F, Shibuya 3-18-5, Shibuya-ku, Tokyo
Phone: +81-3-3498-9080
Hours: 19:00-5:00

Credit: roomie.jp

If you are bored with shopping, eating, drinking and singing, you can always visit the local cinema plaza (*Toho Cinemas*), the *Taito Game* arcades to take purikura (explanation later), the bowling and billiard area at *Shibuya EST*, or just walk around and take in the street art while listening to sidewalk jam sessions. If you are lucky enough, you might be able to discover a few pieces done by the world-renowned Japanese artist, 281_Anti nuke.

If you enjoy playing more serious sports, you can reserve a futsal court for you and your friends at the *Adidas Futsal Park* on the roof of the Tokyu Department Store's Western Building, or join a tournament (More information on their website: http://www.adidas-futsalpark.com/).

Credit: flickr, Curt Smith

What is "purikura", you ask?

Credit: flickr, Laurent Neyssensas

The name itself comes from "Print Club", a series of fun self-shot machines created by Atlus Company in 1995, which became extremely popular in the end of the 90's. Nowadays there are many other companies producing purikura machines and they are quite common to visit after eating out and drinking with friends/co-workers, even for adults. By the way, the biggest purikura store in Japan is also in Shibuya, equipped with as many as 17 machines (*Purikura Shop NOA*).

For music lovers, *Shibuya Club Quattro* is highly recommended. Here you can see both local and international artists in a relatively small arena, where the stage is just an arm's length away (for the schedule, visit http://www.club-quattro.com/shibuya/schedule/).

If you happen to miss the last train after all these fun activities (which happens more frequently than you would imagine), don't worry. You can always stay at one of the manga kissas (manga cafés in English) near the station, where you basically just rent a tiny private cubicle with a computer and a couch/bed. You can spend the night for 2-3 thousand yen, while reading as many manga as you want, watching movies or surfing the net. Of course, you are more than welcome to sleep as well, if you feel like it.

Credit: flickr, Banalities

Once you have discovered Central Shibuya, it is time to venture out a bit more into the diverse neighborhoods.

Harajuku

You can simply walk (18 minutes) or take the JR Yamanote Line (2 minutes, 140 yen) from Shibuya. During the Edo Period, this area was full of samurai residences. In the Meiji Period noblemen lived here. In 1964, Tokyo Olympics was partly (swimming, basketball, etc.) held at the Yoyogi National Gymnasium, which is only a few minutes away. After the opening of *Mademoiselle Nonnon* boutique in 1966, Harajuku became the fashion and youth (sub)culture center of Tokyo. Nowadays you can find teenagers walking or sitting around representing various styles: kawaii, lolita goth, cosplay, etc., especially on Takeshita-dori. You should also visit Harajuku-dori and Shibuyagawa-hodoro (nickname: Cat Street), which are collectively called "Urahara" (literally: back side of Harajuku). Here you can find all the smaller and cheaper shops that could not afford to open a store on the expensive Takeshita-dori.

Credit: flickr, tim t.

Meiji Shrine

Credit: Gergo Sastyin

After you have finished visiting Harajuku, you can make your way towards the Meiji Shrine, which can be approached directly from the JR Harajuku Station in a few minutes. In this shrine, Emperor Meiji and Empress Shoken are worshipped. Its peaceful and breathtaking forest consists of approximately 10 thousand trees, which were donated from all over the country. The forest has grown into a 70 thousand square meter area, providing the visitors not only with a calming atmosphere, but also with many sport and museum facilities as well as a gorgeous location for weddings. This shrine receives most of its visitors at New Year's during hatsu-mode or hatsu-mairi, which is generally done right after midnight, but can extend until the 3rd day of January. This is when they thank the gods for the past year, and pray for the success and happinness of the new year. The number of people visiting here during the first 3 days of the new year is more than 3 million. The shrine is open between 5-6:00 and 17-18:00 (depending on the season). The garden, which includes flowers originally planted by the emperor as a present to the empress, opens a bit later and closes a bit earlier, and can be observed for 500 yen. After visiting the main shrine building, you should keep walking north until you reach a museum called Homotsuden. Here you can find many personal items of the emperor and the empress, as well as temporary exhibitions. It is usually open from 9:00 until 16:00. The entrance fee is also 500 yen.

Speaking of weddings, in Japan, there are generally three types of weddings (although one can do more than one type): kyokai-shiki, shinzen-shiki and jinzen-shiki. Kyokai-shiki is a Christian inspired church wedding that involves wearing a typical white wedding dress and a black suit, regardless of whether or not the couple is Christian. Shinzen-shiki is a wedding in a Shinto shrine wearing a kimono, whereas jinzen-shiki has no limitations to location or clothes. In Japan there is a growing tendency to have a kyokai-shiki wedding, due to western cultural influences.

Yoyogi Park

Credit: Wikipedia

The southern part of this gigantic green area is called Yoyogi Park, where the Olympic Village used to be in 1964. It is a perfect spot for a picnic, to play sports, or simply hang out with friends. This green space full of ponds, fountains and trees is currently the fifth biggest of its kind within the 23 Special Wards. You can also visit the only remaining house from the Olympic Village, where a Dutch athlete used to stay. Occasionally, there are also various international, beer/gourmet festivals, and flee markets held in this park.

Omotesando

Credit: flickr. Ari Helminen

This is an area between Shibuya and Harajuku, slightly to the east. The main walking street, Aoyama-dori extends from Omotesando Station all the way to Shibuya Station. Omotesando has been formed by the contrast between the traditional Japanese atmosphere of Meiji Shrine, and its antonym Harajuku, which is a hub for westernism. However, unlike Harajuku, here, the main influence has been the foreign gourmet, especially French. Therefore it is not surprising that you can find the biggest variety of French cuisine in Omotesando. That being said, there are also quite a few Italian, Spanish and Central European restaurants. I would recommend the Austrian *Cafe Landtmann* for dinner and the Hungarian *Gerbeaud* for dessert, if you have not yet been to those countries.

Cafe Landtmann
Address: Ao Bldg. 4F, Kitaaoyama 3-11-7, Minato-ku, Tokyo
Phone: +81-3-3498-2061
Hours: 11:00-23:00 (Mon. – Sat.), 11:00-22:00 (Sun. and national holidays)

Gerbeaud
Address: Ao Bldg. 2F, Kitaaoyama 3-11-7, Minato-ku, Tokyo
Phone: +81-3-3499-0099
Hours: 11:00-23:00 (Mon. – Sat.), 11:00-22:00 (Sun. and national holidays)

Daikanyama

A gorgeous neighborhood in the southern part of the Shibuya Ward. You can get there from central Shibuya by using the Tokyu Toyoko Line (3 minutes, 130 yen) or on foot (17 minutes). Almost every weekend there are food and handcraft markets on the two main streets: Kyuu-Yamate-dori and Hachiman-dori (for more information: http://weekend-daikanyama.com/). Daikanyama is honestly the perfect place to arrange business or academic meetings. It is not only beautifully and simplistically designed, but also calm, making it easy to hold a conversation. The most beautiful *Tsutaya* store is also here. *Tsutaya* was born in Osaka City in 1983 as a book, music and movie retail shop, and over the years it has started to operate as a movie rental as well. However, the youth of the time grew up and Tsutaya decided to dedicate the Daikanyama store to them with a more mature theme. It has won the grand prize at the 2012 World Architecture Festival in the Best Shopping Center category, and at the 2012 Design For Asia (most prestigious design award in Asia). It has been also chosen into "The 20 Most Beautiful Bookstores in the World" list by Favorwire, a popular NY-based cultural website. It was opened in 2011 and is usually referred to as "T-Site". There are many temporary exhibitions here, as well as talks with artists and academicians (for more information: https://tsite.jp/daikanyama/event/).

Credit: flickr, 淳平 箸井

Shinjuku

A quick history lesson about Shinjuku

Now that you know where Shibuya is, you will have no problem finding Shinjuku, as it is located only 3 stations to the north of Shibuya on the Yamanote Line (7 minutes, 160 yen). Its name comes from the 17th century (Edo Period), when a certain number of lodgings ("yado" or "shuku" in Japanese) were required for each of the five main roads ("kaido") running through the country. On the Koshu-kaido, the first lodging after Nihonbashi (the beginning point of all the five roads, located in Edo/Tokyo) was a bit too far; therefore the local village headman requested a closer one to be built. It was called Naito-Shinjuku as it was placed inside the Naito clan's premises ("shin" means "new" in Japanese, and "juku" is just "shuku", but voiced). The ward itself was created by merging some areas around the main station in 1947 and also named after the station. It suffered great damage in 1945 during the Great Tokyo Air Raid, in which 90% of the houses were destroyed and its population declined to 20% of the original 400 thousand. Since then, however, the ward has seen modernization and development to an incredible extent.

Credit: Wikimedia, Fboas

Credit: Wikimedia, David.Monniaux

After the Tokyo Metropolitan Government headquarters moved here from Marunouchi in 1991, this area became the so-called "new center" of Tokyo. Most of the people from outside the 23 Special Wards come here to work, thus Shinjuku serves as a bridge between central and western Tokyo. This is by far the most active area in Japan. Projections show that by 2020, its daytime population will be over 800 thousand, which will make it the most crowded ward in the capital. No wonder, then, that most of the foreigners in Tokyo live here as well, a total of 37 thousand registered aliens.

This ward has the biggest density of malls, *McDonalds'* and *Uniqlos* in all of Japan. You must have heard of *Uniqlo* already, although perhaps you do not know that it is from Japan. *Uniqlo* is a clothing apparel company, founded in 1949 in Yamaguchi Prefecture. Currently, they have as many as 1,400 stores worldwide. And truthfully, their heat-tech undershirts and underpants go a long way towards helping you survive the freezing cold winters of Tokyo.

Credit: Wikipedia

The station and its crepes

The Shinjuku Station was opened in 1885. This is currently the busiest station in the world according to the Guinness Book of World Records, with over 3.6 million passengers per day.

Before we move on to our next destination, first you have the try the delicious crepes around the station.

Moa 4 Café
Address: Shinjuku Moa 4th Street, Shinjuku 3-20, Shinjuku-ku, Tokyo (turn right after leaving the Western Gate of Shinjuku Station)

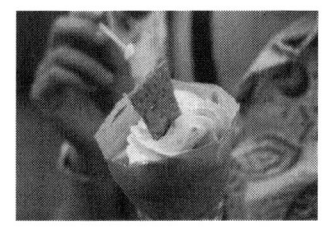

Credit: flckr, L'amande

Petit Barie
Address: Kirin Bldg. 1F, Shinjuku 3-36-2, Shinjuku-ku, Tokyo
Phone: +81-3-3226-3788
Hours: 12:00-23:00

Credit: Wikimedia, Daderot

Shinjuku Gyoen

Another namesake of the ward is Shinjuku Gyoen, a national garden that was opened in 1906. The mansion of the Naito clan used to be here during the Edo Period. Although it was designed as a garden for the imperial family, it was opened to the public after World War II. Within its approximately 58-hectare area, there is a Japanese garden, an English-style landscape garden and a French-style plane-geometrical garden. There are also over 1,300 cherry trees, which makes it an ideal place for hanami (you can find more details about this in the chapter about Ueno) in the beginning of April. Between November 1 and 15, you can also enjoy the view of the beautiful chrysanthemums, which are the symbol of the imperial family (you may remember this from the title of Ruth Benedict's famously biased book, *The Chrysanthemum and the Sword*). It is generally open between 9:00 and 16:00, and the entry fee is 200 yen. It is only 10 minutes walking from Shinjuku Station.

Credit: pixabay, AllAnd

Let's go to the Tokyo Toy Museum!

A three-story building with over 10,000 toys for both children and their parents to enjoy from about 100 different countries. Don't worry, the staff is there to help you to figure out how to play with them. There are also toy making workshops throughout the week (free on weekdays and 1,000 yen on weekends). The entrance fee is 500 yen for children, 700 yen for adults, but only 1,000 for a child-adult duo. Just don't forget to bring some onigiri with you for lunch (typical Japanese snack, a rice ball with some sort of filling) so you can spend the whole day playing!

Credit: flickr, Kentaro Ohno

Tokyo Toy Museum
Address: Yotsuya Hiroba, Yotsuya 4-20, Shinjuku-ku, Tokyo (6 minutes walk from Shinjuku Gyoen)
Phone: +81-3-5367-9601
Hours: 9:00-16:00

If you are still hungry, you can visit one of the seven *Go! Go! Curry* restaurants in Shinjuku, where they sell giant portions for affordable prices. There is also *Komoro Soba* for the more health-conscious people. Soba, by the way, is a thin noodle made from buckwheat flour, served with either cold or hot soup. Very tasty, but to be honest, not quite as filling.

Takadanobaba
You can either walk here (32 minutes) or take the Yamanote Line from Shinjuku (5 minutes, 140 yen). The first thing you will see after leaving the station behind you is the *BIG BOX* building, which literally looks like a big box. It offers a great variety of sport activities for the visitors, such as bowling, swimming, and tennis.

Credit: flickr, cleverclevergirl

As there are many universities and colleges (e. g., Waseda University) nearby, you can find a satisfying selection of ramen stores among many other cheap food choices near the station.

Did you know that over 1,300 Myanmarese live in this area? Frankly, I was quite surprised myself. They live in Little Yangon, north of the station, and their restaurants are most certainly worth a try.

You can also visit the Japan Braille Library (Nihon Tenji Toshokan, or Nitten for short), which was founded in 1940 by Honma Kazuo, a blind journalist and enterpreneur. If you notify them beforehand, a staff member will guide you around and show you the sound studio for the audio books as well as the braille production room. The tours are on Tuesdays and Fridays, starting at 10:00 and at 13:30.

Kabuki-cho

If you are not yet exhausted from all the sightseeing and playing, you should definitely see the (in)famous nightlife in the red light and entertainment district, Kabuki-cho, which is just outside the Eastern Gate of Shinjuku Station. You will surely be able to find some of the strangest places here, from a resturant where girls ride dancing/fighting robots, to a submarine themed (literally) underground bar, all the way to the extremely narrow "Memory Lane" (formerly known as "Piss Alley", I suppose the reason for the change is quite obvious), where you will soon forget about concepts such as a personal space (if you have not already while riding the train/metro during rush hour).

Credit: Wikimedia, Kakidai

Robot Restaurant
Address: Shinjuku Robot Bldg. B2F, Kabuki-cho 1-7-1, Shinjuku-ku, Tokyo
Phone: +81-50-5869-5074 (for reservations only)
Remark: The entrance fee is 6,000 yen. There are four performances every evening.

Dining Bar Submarine
Address: Pocket Bldg. B1, Kabuki-cho 1-17-4, Shinjuku-ku, Tokyo
Phone: +81-3-5285-3480
Hours: 17:00-23:00

The Memory Lane (or Omoide-yokocho in Japanese) is easily accessible from the Eastern Gate of Shinjuku Station. Just walk towards the gigantic ALTA sign, then before crossing the street, enter a sketchy pedestrian underpass on your left, which will bring you directly to this tiny street with more than 80 bars and restaurants on it.

Ikebukuro

Credit: Wikipedia

What's in the name?
Let's go northwest on the Yamanote Line to reach the Ikebukuro Station. While the name of the station literally means "pound bag", in reality, the name originates from the old geographical feature of this land, where many lakes used to lie. So in this case, "fukuro" means a land surrounded by water, and not a bag.

Due to the phonological similarity of the words bag and owl in Japanese (the former is "fukuro" and the latter "fukurō"), you will surely bump into quite a few owl-themed works of art, both inside and outside the station. Among these, the most famous is a stone statue near the Eastern Gate, (very craftily) called "Ikefukurō". This is a major meeting point around here, much like the Hachiko Statue in front of Shibuya Station. It was installed in 1987, when Japan Railways (JR) was born, taking over Japanese National Railways through privatization. Three baby owls were also very recently added to the figure.

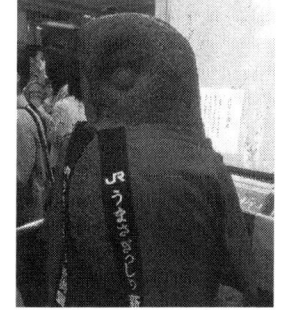

Credit: flickr, hirotomo t

Ikebukuro area is home to the Kyokuto-kai, a peddler-type yakuza faction. There was even a Japanese TV show about them, *Ikebukuro West Gate Park*, which was aired in 2000. The group was established in 1990 and currently has about 1200 members.

Ikebukuro Sunshine City

Credit: Wikimedia, MGA73bot2

In the center of Sunshine City stands a 239.7-meter tall skyscraper, Sunshine 60, which used to be the tallest building in Asia back when it was completed in 1978. Moreover, its indoor observatory, located on the 60th floor, was the highest of its kind until they built Tokyo Skytree in 2011. It also had an observatory on the roof, however, after two suicides it has been closed to the public. Since the 70's an unbelievable number of facilities have been added around this building: more offices and retail stores, a hotel, an aquarium, two indoor theme park (*Namja Town* and *J-World Tokyo*), a planetarium, a theater, a convention hall, and even apartment buildings. According to statistics from 2007, the center has been receiving over 30 million visitors annually.

Namco, the same company that created the arcade game Pac-Man in 1980, possibly one of the most famous games ever, owns the attraction center *Namja Town*. Within *Namja Town*, among many other fun things, you can find food areas with various themes. *Gyoza Stadium* is the place to visit if you are looking for the best savory dumplings. Besides the regular gyoza filled with pork and vegetable, there are also ones containing seafood or cheese, for example. This does sound very exciting, but please make sure to leave some space in your second stomach ("betsubara" in Japanese) for a delicious and slightly shocking dessert experience. By the way, the mechanism of the second stomach has recently been investigated by a Japanese gastroenterologist, Koyama Shigeki, and his results show that the visual stimulus of a dessert can, in fact, cause the stomach to make room for the subsequent feast.

Credit: flickr, isolethetv

After sampling the gyoza, your next destination must be *Fukubukuro Dessert Yokocho*. Within this, you should head directly to the *Gotochi Ice Parlor*. They have about 50 different flavors of ice cream, from which you can choose 6 to put on your plate. Besides the run-of-the-mill apple or peach, you will certainly find the lavender and the tulip flavors more interesting. Although this shop does not draw the line there, those who are braver can experiment with the miso ramen, eel, oyster, Hokkaido potato and curry flavors. Not wild enough for you? Ask for their garlic and wasabi ice creams. The total price starts from 360 yen, but it can be higher depending on your choices.

Credit: flickr, Guilhem Vellut

The entrance fee into *Namja Town* is 500 yen for adults (although some attractions cost extra) and it is open between 10:00 and 22:00.

After this you should see *J-World Tokyo*, especially if you are a fan of Japanese comics and cartoons. Here you can explore the world of Naruto, One Piece and Dragon Ball. It costs 800 yen to enter for adults, from 9:00 to 18:00.

Credit: flickr, Karl Baron

Kit Kat Chocolatory
Not enough weird flavors? You might want to visit the *Kit Kat Chocolatory* inside the Seibu Ikebukuro Station. Japanese people are big fans of this snack, which might have something to do with the fact that Kit Kat sounds a bit like "kitto katsu", meaning "(I will) definitely win". Here you can stimulate your taste buds with purple potato, cinnamon cookie, cheese, bean or wasabi flavored

chocolates. And this is not the end of the list. There are three special flavors, developed by a Japanese chocolatier, Takagi Yasumasa: Sublime Bitter, Special Sakura Green Tea and Special Chilli. Bon appetite!

Rikkyo University (St. Paul's University)

A private Christian university in west Ikebukuro, only a 10-minute stroll from the station. Initially they taught English and Bible Studies here, when it was opened in 1874 as Rikkyo School. Channing Moore Williams, who happened to be one of the first protestant missionaries visiting Japan in the 19th century, founded the school. Later, in 1866, he became the consecrated Bishop for both Japan and China. The university has many beautiful buildings made out of red brick and although it is unfortunately usually closed to the public, you can still sneak a peek from outside. Or you can wait until August, when they open their gates for prospective students.

Credit: Wikimedia, LERK

Otsuka

A 24 minutes walk from Ikebukuro Station or a 3-minute ride on the Yamanote Line (140 yen). You will be surprised by how calm this neighborhood is, despite its proximity to the busy Ikebukuro. You will probably also notice that you can actually breathe in some fresh air here and move around without colliding with anyone. The perfect time to visit is at sunset, when the orange lights so breathtakingly emphasize the nostalgic streets and little shops. It is as if you went back in time to the peaceful late Showa Period.

Otsuka Park

20 minutes walk south, near the Shin-Otsuka Station, you will find yourself in this relatively small park. Let's take a break here and observe the statue of a young boy performing gymnastics (or being apprehended, depending on how you choose to see it). According to some people, the rajio taiso (radio calisthenics) gatherings that were organized here starting in 1929, were the first in the country, although the Sakuma Park and the Miyagawa Square, both in Chiyoda Ward, are also competing for the same title. Speaking of radio taiso, it is still broadcasted on NHK (Japan B roadcasting Corporation) every morning.

Credit: Wikimedia, 夏目・龍之介

Gokoku-ji Temple
After you have rested sufficiently in the park, it is time to continue walking southwest until you reach the magnificent 17th century Gokoku-ji Temple. It was built in 1681, and, has survived all the earthquakes and wars to date, giving us a rather unique opportunity to view an important Buddhist temple from the Edo Period. By the way, Okuma Shigenobu, a politician and founder of Waseda University, and field marshal Yamagata Aritomo are buried here.

Credit: Wikimedia, Lombroso

Ueno

Where is Ueno?
In Bunkyo Ward, the cultural, historical and academic center of Tokyo. It came into existence in 1948, after being home to many samurai houses in the Edo Period, then universities and military zones in the Meiji Period. Mori Ogai, Natsume Soseki, Higuchi Ichiyo, and Ishikawa Takuboku all lived here, just to name a few very well-known and influential authors. It is no exaggeration to say that Bunkyo Ward was the birthplace of modern Japanese literature. It is currently home to a large number of artists, reporters, editors, and scientists.

It takes 27 minutes to get here from Shinjuku Station on the Yamanote Line (200 yen). It is also accessible on foot, but not recommended as it takes an hour and 43 minutes (that is, unless you are prepared to walk much more after that).

Ueno Station
There really isn't anything to explore at the station, with the possible exception of the giant statue of a panda locked inside a transparent plastic box. So, after getting a glimpse of the statue, you should make your way out of the building as soon as possible and visit the Ameyoko shopping street. It is always quite busy, but you will surely appreciate the old-time charm of this neighborhood. Besides the various street foods such as fish and fruits (make sure that you check out *Hyakkaen*), you can also enjoy many traditional Japanese performing arts such as rakugo (comical story-telling). For rakugo, comedy, acrobatics and much more, visit the most historic entertainment hall in Tokyo: *Suzuimoto Engeijo*.

Credit: Gergo Sastyin

Suzuimoto Engeijo
Address: Suzumoto Bldg. 3F, Ueno 2-7-12, Taito-ku, Tokyo

Phone: +81-3-3834-5906

Other recommendations include *Kadokura*, a bar/restaurant with amazing hamukatsu (ham cutlet), and *Usagiya*, a shinise (a traditional store that has been run by the same family for many generations) Japanese confectionary, founded in 1913.

Kadokura
Address: Forum-aji Bldg. 1F, Ueno 6-13-1, Taito-ku, Tokyo
Phone: +81- 3-3832-5335
Hours: 10:00-23:30

Usagiya
Address: Ueno 1-10-10, Taito-ku, Tokyo
Phone: +81-3-3831-6195
Hours: 9:00-18:00

Ueno Park
Ueno Park is an enormous garden that stretches between Ueno Station and The University of Tokyo. This was the first area to be designated as a park in Japan, with a history dating back to as early as 1873. Originally it was designed as a garden for the Kanei-ji Temple (built in 1625), however it was transferred to state property after the Meiji Restoration, then to Tokyo City in 1924. It is without doubt the best spot for hanami (see below). It has been that way since the late Edo Period, when hundreds of cherry trees were planted here. Approximately 2 million people visit the park every spring during hanami season, to enjoy picnics enveloped in over a thousand blooming cherry trees.

Credit: Gergo Sastyin

If you are wondering about the statue near the southern entrance of the park, it depicts Saigo Takamori, a 19th century warrior and politician, and it was unveiled in 1898. The dog on his right was his beloved Samoyed, Tsun, and they are on their way to a rabbit hunt. Saigo was one of the Three Great Nobles, who contributed to the overthrow of the Tokugawa Shogunate and the start of the Meiji Restoration, in order to transform Japan into a more open and modern country.

The park is open between 5:00 and 23:00, and free to enter. It is right next to the Ueno Station, so you really cannot miss it.

Hanami

Literally means "flower viewing" and is by far the most magical season in Japan (the second one would be momiji, the season of autumn leaves). During hanami, practically everyone living in the country goes to the parks with cherry trees (or "sakura" in Japanese) and enjoys the stunning views along with food and lots and lots of alcohol. In fact, most of the time they are more interested in the consumption part than in the flower viewing itself. There is even a Japanese proverb, "Hana yori dango" (rice dumplings over flowers) that expresses this sentiment. The blue plastic mats lying around the park need to be reserved well ahead in time, especially if you are planning a picnic with a bigger group of friends or co-workers. Otherwise, you can always find an unoccupied patch of grass for yourself or a couple of people to lie down and simply take in the beauty of the flowers.

Credit: Gergo Sastyin

Credit: Gergo Sastyin

Ueno Zoological Gardens

It was established in 1882, and is considered to be the earliest zoological garden in Japan. Emperor Showa later presented the

Credit: Gergo Sastyin

zoo to Tokyo City in 1924. In 1972, a giant panda was added to the zoo family in order to celebrate the reparation of diplomatic relations between Japan and China. It currently houses about 400 different species, and 3000 animals in total. In the Eastern Park, there are giant pandas (Lili and Shinshin, who arrived to the zoo in 2011), gorillas, tigers, bears, and seals. In the Western Park, you can see giraffes, hippos, rhinos, aye-ayes, shoebills, and many amphibians and reptiles. It is generally open between 9:30 and 17:00, and the entrance fee is 600 yen for adults (closed on Mondays).

Tokyo National Museum

The Tokyo National Museum was also the very first of its kind in Japan. So many firsts, I know... But as I said, this *is* the historical center of Tokyo. The museum opened in 1872, although it only moved to Ueno Park in 1882. It is the home of 87 pieces of national treasure and 633 important cultural properties (115,653 artworks in total, plus 2,519 consigned items). Among these, 200-300 pieces are usually open to viewing. The museum complex consists of six separate buildings, amongst which Hon-kan (the main building), Hyokei-kan and Kuroda Memorial Hall are the most impressive from the outside.

Hon-kan was completed in 1938, and is still one of the best examples of Japanese-Western hybrid architecture. It exhibits countless objects of art from the ancient Jomon Period to the 19th century, including Buddhist statues, tea ceremony artifacts, samurai equipment, folding screen

Credit: Gergo Sastyin

and sliding door paintings, noh and kabuki masks, ukiyo-e prints, swords and ceramics.

Hyokei-kan (see the photo on the left) is the oldest building of the museum, and was opened in 1909 to honor the wedding of Crown Prince Taisho. It is currently closed for an indefinite period for maintenance and restoration.

Credit: Gergo Sastyin

The construction of the Kuroda Memorial Hall was built at the bequest of a western-style painter, Kuroda Seiki, whose paintings and other artistic endeavors are displayed here. The building was completed in 1928, and in 1930 it opened its doors as The Institute of Arts Research for the Imperial Academy of Fine Arts.

Although the rest of the buildings are less impressive from the outside, their exhibitions could nevertheless be worth a visit. The Toyo-kan, which features art and historical collections from all over Asia, including Korea, China, Southeast and Central Asia, India and Egypt, is amongst the more impressive collections.

The admission fee to the Tokyo National Museum is 620 yen for adults and 410 yen for university students (except for the Kuroda Memorial Hall, which is free to enter). All the exhibitions are open between 9:30 and 17:00.

Kuromon
This architectural piece is also part of the museum, although there is nothing to see inside. The name literally means the "Black Gate" and it used to be located at the residence of the Ikeda feudal family. Considering the style and the materials used, it was probably built in the late Edo Period. It was moved near the museum in 1954 from the Crown Prince's villa.

Another similarly famous feudal residence gate is at The University of Tokyo, called Akamon, or "Red Gate".

Shinobazu Pond

This pond is located on the southwest side of the park and it represents the Biwa-ko Lake, the biggest inland body of water in Japan (Shiga Prefecture). On a semi-island within Shinobazu, there is Benten-do, a small Buddhist hall of worship, which was built in the 17th century as part of the Kanei-ji Temple. It is dedicated to Benten (or Benzaiten), the goddess of wisdom and fortune (originally Sarasvati in the Hindu religion).

Credit: Gergo Sastyin

Shinobazu Pond can be divided into three sections: Lotus Pond with its countless lotus plants in the summer; Boat Pond, where you can rent a rowboat or a paddleboat; and Cormorant Pond, for bird lovers. The pond is especially lovely at night, after all the other visitors have left. In fact, if you live nearby, you should go out for a run around midnight, as long as if you do not mind the occasional encounters with bats and homeless people.

The University of Tokyo Hongo Campus

You can easily walk here from Ueno through the park (29 minutes). Unfortunately there is no direct train or metro connection.

The University of Tokyo is Japan's most prestigious university (Tokyo Daigaku, or Todai in short). As of 2015, it ranks 21th in the world and 1st in Asia, according to Times Higher Education. Its history dates back all the way to 1684, when Tenmonkata, an astronomical institution was installed. Other predecessors are the Otamaga-ike Vaccination Institution from 1858, and the Shoheizaka Academy from 1790. In 1877, the first two were merged into The University of Tokyo. The two main campuses are the Hongo Campus in Bunkyo Ward, which is mainly used for research and specialized education, and the Komaba Campus in Shibuya Ward, for general education and liberal arts. The number of Nobel laureates affiliated with the university is 8, only slightly behind Kyoto University.

What to see in the Hongo Campus?

Credit: flickr, Richard, enjoy my life!

First of all, the school has 8 gates in total, among which Akamon or Red Gate is the most famous and worth a visit. It was originally built in 1827 for the Maeda clan and has since been associated with the university itself. You will see dozens of junior high and high school students posing for photographs in front of the gate, so just try to squeeze yourself through the crowd and enter the campus. Now you can imagine how annoying it can be to go to classes there everyday; no wonder that most of the students do not actually use this entrance.

First you should turn left and then right to get to the General Library. The original brick building (built in 1892) was destroyed in the 1923 Great Kanto Earthquake. The current building was built through a donation from the Rockefeller Foundation, and designed by a Japanese architect, Uchida Yoshikazu. The front side looks like a bookshelf with books lining up. Strangely enough, I had not noticed this until now either. Inside, you will see a red carpet covering the stairs, as well as

Credit: Gergo Sastyin

a gorgeous western-style interior with chandeliers and paintings. To visit, you will need to complete a short procedure between 9:00 and 17:00.

Faculty of Law and Letters Building 1, 2 and 3 were designed by Uchida Yoshikazu and completed in the 20's and the 30's, after the Great Kanto Earthquake. Personally, my favorite parts of this complex are the arches that allow you to look through all three buildings if you stand on the northern side of the library. They exhibit carvings similar to those used in ancient Greece, which are one of the main characteristics of the distinctive style called "Uchida Gothic". If you happen to be here in autumn, spend some time on the road that leads from the Main Gate to the Yasuda Auditorium, between the Faculty of Law and Letters Building 1 and 2. The fan-shaped leaves of the gingko trees (or "ginnan" in Japanese) on both sides of this street usually paint everything yellow (although they do smell kind of bad), and they can be also found in the logo of the university. If you are hungry or you feel like having a beer, you can visit the *Ginnan Metro Refectory*, which is an underground cafeteria in Building 2. It is open from 11:00 to 20:00, except for weekends and national holidays.

Credit: Gergo Sastyin

The perfect place to finish our tour at Todai is the small park with a pond in the middle, just next to the General Library. The surrounding area became a garden in 1638 for the Maeda clan and the lake was originally called Shinji-ike, as its shape is reminiscent of the Chinese character "kokoro" (or "shin"). Later it was renamed as Sanshiro-ike, due to an influence from Natsume Soseki's novel, *Sanshiro*, in which the pond serves as the location for the main character's first encounter with a girl, whom he falls in love with.

May Festival

The festival was first held in 1923, and has been organized 88 times so far (as of 2015). Currently, about 500 groups participate annually, and their job is to entertain the over 150 thousand visitors. The groups cook or bake food, serve drinks, do various performances or show you what they have been up to since last year's festival. It is definitely an interesting experience, especially if you want to know more about the local students and their lives.

Okay, admittedly I studied at Todai, so I am a little bit partial, but I am sure you will appreciate the atmosphere this campus has to offer if you choose to visit it.

Ochanomizu

Credit: Gergo Sastyin

It is just a 19 minutes walk from the Akamon to the area called Ochanomizu, or "tea water" in Japanese, a name referencing the Kanda River that flows across the neighborhood. From the Ochanomizu Bridge, you have a wonderful view of the station and the passengers as they wait for the train to arrive. The rails run on the edge of a cliff that follows the river. In front, you will be able to observe another passage over the water, Hijiri Bridge , which was built in 1928. If you come here at night, you will see its beautifully lit arch reflecting on the river, forming a circle. If you keep walking down the main street (the JR station should be on your left), you will find yourself in the largest collection of second-hand music instruments and ski/snowboard equipment shops.

One of my favorite places to eat here is *Napoli no Shitamachi Shokudo*, which serves delicious Italian food in a splendid ambience.

Napoli no Shitamachi Shokudo
Address: New Surugadai Bldg. B1F, Kanda Surugadai 2-1-45, Chiyoda-ku, Tokyo
Phone: +81-50-5571-4199 (for reservation only)
Hours: 11:00-23:00

Tokyo Dome City

17 minutes on foot to the west along the river until Tokyo Dome City, a huge entertainment complex with an amusement park, a stadium for baseball and concerts (Tokyo Dome), restaurants and shops. The Big O, a giant ferris wheel, provides the visitors with an exceptional view of the area

Credit: flickr, Kentaro Ohno

for 820 yen. You can even choose the background music for your 15 minutes ride! By the way, this is world's biggest centerless wheel with its 60-meter diameter. The Thunder Dolphin rollercoaster, the largest of its kind in Tokyo, passes through the center of the wheel.

Koraku-en

Credit: Wikimedia, Fjkelfeinvvn

Finally, I believe it is time to rest a little bit in the Koishikawa Koraku-en Garden, which can be reached within 2 minutes from the Tokyo Dome City. It is a very successful mix of Japanese and Chinese garden techniques, where the plum season (mid-February through March), the hanami season and the momiji season (late November and early December) are all equally enjoyable. Look for the red Tsuten-kyo Bridge!

Akihabara & Asakusa

The history of "autumn leaf field"
One station away on the Yamanote Line from Ueno (4 minutes, 140 yen) or a 22 minutes walk straight south. Welcome to the otaku mecca, Akihabara (or Akiba, in short)! Literally, the name means "autumn leaf field". There are many unknown details about the actual history of this name, although the gist of it can be summarized as follows: There was a big fire in 1869 and the disaster destroyed about 1,100 houses. In fact, such fires were so frequent at the time that Edo, the capital back then, was even called the the "City of Fires". Thus, they decided to leave the current area of Akihabara empty for fire fighting purposes. Later on, as an added measure against fires, they built Chinka-jinja (fire prevention shrine) here. The people, however, believed that it was the shrine of Akiha Daigongen, the most prominent god of fire prevention, thus they began to call it Akiha-jinja, and after a while the area itself was known as Akihano-hara, Akihaga-hara, or Akihappara. The name remained inconsistent until the local station started to accept passenger trains as well as cargo trains, when the name "Akihabara" stuck.

Electric Town
Despite the general opinion on the area, Akihabara is not only for geeks (or otakus in Japanese). Virtually anyone living in our modern society – unless you are a technophobe – can probably find something of interest to them at Akihabara. This is because, besides all the otaku stores you may encounter here (more details on that in a moment), you can also find the world's largest selection of cheap but still extremely high-quality electronics, such as cameras, TVs, computers, vacuum cleaners, and basically anything you can imagine, as well as quite a few things that you probably never even conceived of.

The colossal Yodobashi Camera store, which has become a symbolic building of Akihabara, is right at the Central Gate of the station. Yodobashi Camera was founded in 1960 and as the name suggests, it used to exclusively sell cameras and

Credit: flickr, MIKI Yoshihito

photography-related products. Since then it has developed into one of Japan's representative establishments that sells all sorts of electronic items (to be precise, the 5th biggest in terms of sales after Yamada Denki, Bic Camera, Edion and K's Holdings). Currently it has 21 shops nation-wide, and Yodobashi Akiba is the second biggest among all (the biggest one is in Umeda, Osaka). The staff has detailed and extensive knowledge about every single product, and many of them speak English as well, so feel free to ask them any questions you may have about whatever you are looking for. It also has collectible figures and cards on the 6th floor, as well as a golf practice range and batting cages on the 9th floor. The store hours are from 9:30 to 20:00, while the golf range and batting cages are open between 10:30 and 23:00.

If you are not satisfied with the prices you get at this store, don't give up: there are a million and one other places you can visit, such as Sofmap, Yamada Denki and Llaox. Duty-free stores such as AKKY are also an option, as some of the items sold in other stores may be designed for use within Japan only. However, if you choose to shop at a duty-free store, please keep in mind the following requirements: you must show your passport, you must purchase over the amount of 10,001 yen, and you must have arrived in Japan less than 6 months before your purchase.

Between the station and Chuo-dori (central street), there is the Akihabara Radio Center, where the Akihabara "Electric Town" began in 1945. After World War II, electronics and radio engineers gathered here in an attempt to sell radio parts

Credit: Wikimedia, Ken OHYAMA

and other electronic junk. There are currently 38 tiny retailers in the center, selling all sorts of cables, plugs, measuring instruments, switches, and other electronic components. If you are into DIY, or you need specific pieces for a device you already own, this is where you should go.

Geek Capital

Credit: flickr, Ryo FUKAsawa

The other half of Akihabara consists of cafes and shops targeting fans of games, animes and mangas, as well as the subculture of J-pop and kawaii stuff. Some of you might already be familiar with these concepts, and for the rest of you, I strongly recommend looking into them before sightseeing, so that you will have a general idea of what to expect. The worldwide market of Japanese mangas, animes and games is a several hundred billion dollars industry. It is quite usual for a manga story become an anime, a TV show or a movie (or, more often than not, a combination of these), then be made into video games, and bring with it a slew of card games (we all remember Pokémon cards, don't we?), collectible figures and other goods. Akihabara is absolutely worth a visit, even if you are not completely obsessed with any of these phenomena, as it provides a unique opportunity to get completely immersed in (or possibly drown in) a very prominent aspect of modern Japanese culture.

Anime/Manga

Mandarake is an 8-floor building full of items related to anime, manga, cosplay and so on, close to the Denkigai Gate of the station (hours: 12:00-20:00). Don't forget to check out their floor of customizable dolls, especially if it has been a while since you have had nightmares. And, if you can't get all your shopping done at the store, they have an online store as well.

Gundam Café is (as you can probably guess) a café dedicated entirely to the Mobile Suit Gundam anime series, which essentially created the robot anime genre in the end of the 70's. The interior design and the staff uniform is already enough to make you feel like you stepped into the world of Gundam, but even the food and the drinks have the shapes of certain characters (a little too much maybe?).

Credit: flickr, Manuel Menal

Gundam Cafe
Address: Kanda Hanaoka-cho 1-1, Chiyoda-ku, Tokyo
Phone: +81-3-3251-0078
Hours: 10:00-22:30

Toys/Games
For second-hand collectibles, look for *Liberty*, which owns 13 stores scattered around in Akihabara, amongst which Building 8 has the biggest selection. They are generally open between 11:00 and 20:00.

For serious collectors of nostalgic TV and computer games, your best bet is *Super Potato*, although it may sound more like a grocery store (general hours: 11:00-20:00). If you find their prices too high, you can always go back to *Mandarake*, as they also sell games (general hours: 11:00-20:00).

After an exhausting day of hunting, have a beer at *A-Button*, where you can enjoy the retro arcade atmosphere, while playing old-school games with your friend or a local.

A-Button
Address: 5th Kosei Bldg. 1F, Taito 1-13-9, Taito-ku, Tokyo
Phone: +81-3-5856-5475
Hours: 20:00-4:00

Maid Cafés

You are about to enter possibly the strangest world of Akihabara, where the waitresses (or waiters, depending on your inclinations) are dressed up in various costumes and literally ready to serve you. This includes waiting on your table, but for some extra fee, you can play rock-paper-scissors with them (be careful, there might be punishment for the loser!), or get spoon fed, and receive grooming, as well as massages. The general rule is that taking photos is absolutely prohibited, unless you can make an agreement with someone, for an extra fee of course.

Credit: Wikimedia, Szater

Shinobazu Café (with girls dressed as ninja warriors)
Address: Watanabe Bldg. 3F, Soto-Kanda 1-8-6, Chiyoda-ku, Tokyo
Phone: +81-3-3525-4018
Hours: 17:00-22:00 (weekdays), 15:00-22:00 (weekends and national holidays)

Tsundere, the latest trend in maid cafés, was influenced by animes such as *Kimi ga Nozomu Eien*, where the girls are unpredictable, cold and quite mean, although they can become rather clingy after a while. Unfortunately, the only exclusive tsundere-type maid café has recently closed. That being said, you might still be able to catch an event at *Pinafore* (for more details, visit: http://pinafore.jp/en/, or their Facebook page).

Animal Cafés

Who wouldn't like to pet cats or rabbits while lingering over a cup of coffee? If you are not allergic to animals, give them a try (and an occasional belly rub)!

Credit: flickr, John Gillespie

Neko Jalala
Address: Suehiro-cho Heim 1F, Soto-Kanda 3-5-5, Chiyoda, Tokyo
Phone: +81-3-3258-2525
Hours: 11:00-20:00
Remarks: Kitties! 530 yen / 30 minutes + drinks

Candy Fruit Usagi no Yakata
Address: Isuzu Bldg. 9F, Soto-Kanda 4-6-2, Chiyoda, Tokyo
Phone: +81-3-6206-4885
Hours: 14:00-21:30 (weekdays), 12:00-21:30 (weekends and national holidays)
Remarks: Bunnies! 1,100 yen (1,300 yen on weekends) / 30 minutes (unlimited soft drinks)

J-Pop

Credit: flickr, kndynt2099

If you mix J-Pop with Akihabara, you get AKB48, a popular girl band. Although, as the name suggests, it originally started with 48 members, by 2014 their number had increased to 140. Not surprisingly, their locations are full of middle-aged men in suits, as there is only one thing that is harder to resist for Japanese salarymen (businessmen) than underage girls singing and jumping around in cute uniforms, and that is there being even more of them doing so at once. If you also share their obsession or would like to see salarymen in their natural habitat, visit the *AKB48 café/shop* (right next to *Gundam Café*) or the *AKB48 Theater* (on the 8th floor of the discount retailer, *Don Quijote*).

AKB48 Official Café & Shop
Address: Kanda Hanaoka-cho 1-1, Chiyoda-ku, Tokyo
Phone: +81-3-5297-4848
Hours: 11:00-20:00 (visit their website for more details)

If this was still not enough, at *Dear Stage* you can watch amateur pop idol performances live.

Dear Stage
Address: Dempa Bldg., Soto-Kanda 3-10-9, Chiyoda-ku, Tokyo
Phone: +81-3-5207-9181
Hours: 18:00-22:50 (weekdays), 17:00-22:50 (weekends and national holidays)
Remarks: 3 performances daily on weekdays, and 4 performances on weekends and holidays. The entrance fee is 1,000 yen that includes one drink.

Asakusa

How is Asakusa different from Akihabara? The answer would be, in every possible aspect. Asakusa is one of the best-preserved examples of how the city looked like in the post-war Showa era. At the same time, it can be considered to be a miniature version of Kyoto with its ryokans (Japanese-style inns), jinrikishas (rickshaws, carts pulled by a person) and geishas (exactly 54 of them, at least in 2005). Take the Tsukuba Express train from Akihabara, which will bring you here in 4 minutes and for 210 yen.

Credit: Gergo Sastyin

Where did the name of Asakusa come from? Nobody knows for sure, but it might have originated from Ainu (meaning "crossing the sea"), Tibetan (meaning "sacred land") or standard Japanese (meaning "shallow grass").

When should you come here?
During the Sanja Festival (or Matsuri in Japanese) in May, the Asakusa Samba Carnival in August, or the Hagoita Market in December.

Credit: Wikimedia, Torsodog

Sanja (literally "three gods") Festival was born in 1872, when three separate events were merged into one. It is the annual festival of the Asakusa Shrine, and one of the most representative ones in Japan. During the three days it is organized, as many as 30 groups of men women and children carry around their own mikoshis (portable shrines). There are also floating stages, on which you can witness musicians playing on flutes and drums, as well as dancers. Follow them to the shrine, then watch the performance of the Binzasara Mai traditional dance.

Asakusa Samba Carnival was first organized in 1981 and since then it has become the largest Samba contest on the northern hemisphere. In 2015, 7 S-2 league, and 9 S-1 league teams are planning to compete.

Hagoita is basically a wooden paddle, used with hane (shuttle) as a set to play hanetsuki, a traditional Japanese New Year's game, which bears great resemblance to badminton. At this annual market on Nakamise-dori (see below), you can find hagoitas decorated with kabuki actors and charming Edo ladies, but even Harry Potter or the former Prime Minister, Koizumi Junichiro can sometimes show up in these illustrations.

Credit: Wikimedia, bingabangaboom

68

Buddhism and Shintoism in Asakusa

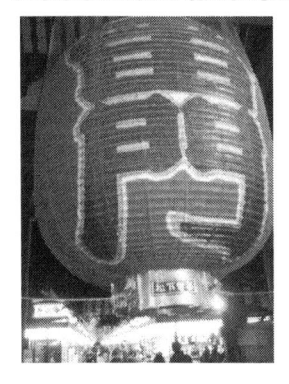

Credit: Gergo Sastyin

The Sensoji Temple and the Asakusa Shrine are the main sites of Asakusa and are right next to each other. Sensouji Temple was built in 645 after three fishermen found a statue of Kannon (the goddess of mercy in Buddhism) in the Sumida River. The three founders are enshrined in the Asakusa Shrine (completed in 1649), which has only become a separate entity after the 1868 Shinbutsu Bunri (Separation of Shintoism and Buddhism) decree. The outer gate of the temple-shrine hybrid is called Kaminari-mon ("Thunder Gate") and can easily be recognized by its giant lantern with the gate's name on it, the two Shinto statues on the sides (Fujin, the god of wind, and Raijin, the god of thunder), its beautiful red color and a large crowd of people struggling to take a photo under the lantern. Beyond this gate, we can find the Nakamise-dori, which is a shopping street stuffed with souvenirs and traditional food stands, leading all the way to the second gate, Hozo-mon. Entering through this gate, we are welcomed by the main hall of Sensoji and a five storied pagoda. Both of them are 20th reconstructions of the originals, which were destroyed in the Great Tokyo Air Raid, but they are nevertheless fascinating, especially at night. The shrine is just a few steps away from here, towards the left.

Credit: Gergo Sastyin

Let's try the Buddhist fortune-telling ("omikuji") here. Find a stand full of drawers. After inserting 100 yen into the slot below (no cheating), pick up the metal box, shake it well, then read the number on the metal stick that comes out of it. Find the drawer corresponding to your number and take one of the sheets of paper inside. It is usually only written in Japanese, but I am sure you can find someone to translate it for you. Good luck!

Tokyo Skytree

Opened in 2012 as a broadcasting tower. With its impressive 634-meters height, this is currently the tallest tower in the world, and the second tallest man-made structure (right after Burj Khalifa at 829.8m). It is also surrounded by restaurants, offices and shopping facilities, forming the Tokyo Skytree Town. The highest observation floor is at 451.2 meters on the 445th (!) floor, which is currently the 4th highest in the world. From here you have a perfect 360 degrees view of the capital.

Credit: Gergo Sastyin

You can buy tickets in advance to go up to the 350 meters observation floor (for adults, 2,570 yen; 2,060 yen at the tower), but the tickets for the 450 meters observation floor must be purchased once you are there (1,030 yen for adults). The decks are open between 8:00 and 22:00 (the last entry is at 21:00). There is also a café and a restaurant on the 350 meters deck, although, if you chose to eat or drink here, be prepared to spend a pretty penny.

Asakusa Engei Hall

Credit: Wikimedia, Kakidai

Everything started in 1907 with a movie theater called Sanyu-kan. After the war in 1951, its site was turned into Furansu-za, a striptease theater, but the organizers shut this down in 1964 and started the Toyo Theater, where, for instance, Kitano "Beat" Takeshi was one of the actors. I am sure you remember him from *HANA-BI* or from *Zatoichi*. On the 4th and 5th floors of the same building, they opened Asakusa Engei Hall in 1964, which has since moved to the ground floor. Besides rakugo, they also have manzai (traditional stand-up comedy) and other genres. It costs 2,800 yen (2,300 yen for students) to enter and you can stay until closing time.

Foooood

Asakusa is mainly known for its yakitori (fried chicken) and tempura (other deep-fried things), so I will recommend a restaurant/bar from each of these categories. *Daikokuya Tempura* was established in 1887 and is especially famous for its tendon (tempura rice bowl).

Daikokuya Tempura
Address: Asakusa 1-38-10, Taito-ku, Tokyo
Phone: +81-3-3844-1111
Hours: 11:10-20:30 (weekdays), 11:10-21:00 (weekends and national holidays)

Asakusa Toriyoshi
Address: Asakusa 1-8-2, Taito-ku, Tokyo
Phone: +81-3-3844-6262
Hours: Lunch is 11:30-14:00, and dinner is 17:00-23:00 (until 22:30 on Saturdays), closed on Sundays

Ginza

Short introduction of Ginza
This is the ultimate shopping district with expensive luxury goods, fancy bars/lounges, lavish hostess clubs and art galleries. It was originally the location of the feudal government's silver molding and issuing agency, back in the Edo Period ("gin" means "silver"). You can easily get here from Asakusa by taking the Ginza Metro Line first to Ueno, then the Yamanote Line. The entire trip will cost you 330 yen. If you did not come here to spend all your life savings, Ginza still has many things to offer to you that are free or relatively cheap.

Walking around Ginza

Credit: Gergo Sastyin

The Ginza Chuo-dori (central street) was the first place in Tokyo, where the Pedestrian's Paradise rule was implemented in 1970. Pedestrian's Paradise allows people to walk on the road without having to worry about cars or bikes on weekends and national holiday, between 12:00 and 18:00 (April-September), or 12:00 and 17:00 (October-March). Akihabara and Shinjuku has also followed Ginza's example, although with a more limited schedule. While wandering on Chuo-dori, pay attention to some of the unique architectural pieces such as the *Mikimoto Boutique*, *Ginza Wako* and *De Beers* building, which looks a bit like the Dancing House in Prague.

Mikimoto was founded in 1893 by Mikimoto Kokichi, a Japanese inventor, who was one of the first creators of cultivated pearls (although the actual method was patented to Nishikawa Tokishi and Mise Tatsuhei). Nevertheless, his company was the one that enabled Japan's pearl business to skyrocket

Credit: Wikimedia, Oiuysdfg

72

and reach a production of 10 million pieces a year. *Mikimoto Boutique* focuses on casual jewelry, but the building itself is already worth a look with its irregular glowing windows.

Credit: Gergo Sastyin

Wako is a department store famous for its main building in Ginza, at the crossing of Chuo-dori and Harumi-dori. Its predecessor was *K. Hattori*, a retail shop selling imported watches and jewelry since 1881 (now: Seiko Holdings Corporation). Since then the clock tower has become the symbol of Ginza and is featured in many movies, including two Godzilla motion pictures. The current neo-renaissance building was completed in 1932 after the Great Kanto Earthquake. At every hour, the Westminster Chimes are played from the tower.

Windows shopping is another popular activity in Ginza, where no display can be too weird. Have a look at *Mitsukoshi*, *Matsuya* and *Tokyu Hands*. The last one is a must-see from the inside as well, particularly for DIY fans, but the large selection of odd items guarantees a fun time for everyone.

If you have not seen a kabuki play before, this might be your best chance, as one of the best theaters in Japan happens to be in Ginza. Kabuki-za Theater was opened in 1889, although it has been rebuilt and renovated several times. It can accommodate almost 2,000 visitors and the tickets are rather affordable.

Credit: Wikimedia, Tak1701d

Ginza turns extraordinarily magical at night, when the streets become colorful canvases due to the hundreds and hundreds of neon signs.

Eating in Ginza
For lunch, I recommend *Ginza Sushidokoro Marui*, where you can have a filling rice bowl-style sushi meal with soup included.

Ginza Sushidokoro Marui
Address: Ginza 3-8-15, Chuo-ku, Tokyo
Phone: +81-3-3564-8601
Lunch hours: 11:30-14:30

For dinner, why not visit one of the restaurants of the trendy "Oreno" series (literally "My [something]"), which serves gourmet food for affordable prices? Unless you cannot stand the idea of standing throughout your meal and having a 2 hours limit for your stay, you will surely be satisfied with *Oreno Italian*. If you definitely want to sit down, reserve early!

Oreno Italian
Address: Ginza 8-6-18, Chuo-ku, Tokyo
Phone: +81-3-6228-5913
Hours: 16:00-23:00 (weekdays and Saturdays), 16:00-22:30 (Sundays and national holidays)

Credit: flickr, Richard, enjoy my life!

I know I said I was not going to discuss anything expensive here, but I just cannot skip Sukiyabashi Jiro. This restaurant has received a 3-star rank from Michelin Guide 8 years in a row and was the subject of the 2011 documentary, Jiro Dreams of Sushi. Quality of course comes with a price: it costs 30,000 yen to have a meal here and you need to reserve your seat at least a month ahead.

Hibiya
A 7-minute walk on the Harumi-dori towards the Imperial Palace will take us to Hibiya, a neighborhood between Hibiya Park and Yurakucho. This area is the birthplace of Toho

Company, a major Japanese filmmaker and distributor. On the northern side of *Hibiya Chanter*, look for the tiny Godzilla statue. This square is also covered with the handprints of famous movie stars.

Hibiya Park is a perfectly relaxing place to have a picnic or just pick up a book and lie down somewhere near the fountain.

Credit: Gergo Sastyin

Yuraku-cho

Credit: Photozou, Rubber Soul

If you are looking for something to eat or drink, just head towards the elevated tracks of the Yamanote Line in either direction from Yuraku-cho. You will find a countless number of bars and restaurants on both sides of the rails. This kind of area is called "gado-shita" or "under the girders".

Yurakucho is also known for its convention and exhibition center, the Tokyo International Forum, which consists of several halls, a museum, a restaurant and many other facilities. Hall A is currently the second largest concert hall in the world with its capacity to seat 5,012 people (after Radio City Music Hall of New York). The ship-themed Glass Building is also worth seeing.

Credit: Gergo Sastyin

Tsukiji Market

Only 5 minutes from Hibiya on the Hibiya Metro Line (170 yen). Here you can witness the largest (in terms of money transaction; the Ota Market actually has a larger surface area) fish market in the world. In 2015 alone, the transactions amounted to approximately 916,866 tons and 6 hundred billion yen. Its history goes back to the 1930's and is likely to end in 2016, when they are planning to move the market to another location in Toyosu.

Credit: flickr, Anna & Michal

The Tsukiji Market is made up of an inside and an outside area. The tuna auction and the wholesale market, which are the most popular attractions here, take place in the inner market. There are many restaurants both inside and outside the building. The maximum number of visitors at the tuna auction is 120 per day. They are separated into two groups: the first group is admitted between 5:25 and 5:50 in the morning, the second between 5:50 and 6:15. Make sure that you go there early enough (before 5 o'clock) and apply at the Osakana Fukyu Center near the Kachidoki Gate. The wholesale market area can be only accessed after 9:00, because most of the business is conducted prior to that. Do not bring big suitcases, children or pets, and always be careful not to block the traffic. Have a fresh sushi breakfast or lunch while you are there!

Imperial Palace

The Imperial Palace

Credit: flickr, Stéfan

Formerly the location of the Edo Castle, the residence of Tokugawa shoguns, between 1603 and 1867. The Edo Castle was renamed as Tokyo Castle in 1868, when Emperor Meiji visited from Kyoto and thus began the Meiji Restoration. The next year, in 1869, it was again renamed as the Imperial Castle. In 1888 the Meiji Palace was completed, although it was destroyed in 1945 in air raids. In 1948, the area ceased to be referred to as a "castle" and from that time on they only called it as "Kokyo" or "the Imperial Residence" (although in English its official name is still the "Imperial Palace"). In 1968, the construction of a new palace was completed and is currently being used for formal events. Their Majesties the Emperor and the Empress are living in a building in Kokyo named "Gosho". Kokyo's postal code is 100-0001 and its total area including all the surrounding parks adds up to 1,150,000 km². The Imperial Palace (Kokyo) consists of four main areas: the inner grounds, the East Gardens, the Outer Gardens, and the Kitanomaru Park (this is where you can find the Nippon Budokan, the Science Museum and the National Museum of Modern Art).

From the Outer Gardens, you can see a double-arched stone bridge, which is the Seimon-ishibashi ("main gate stone bridge"). Seimon-tetsubashi ("main gate iron bridge") is right behind this. It is also known as Niju-bashi (double or two-fold bridge), because it used to have two levels until 1964, when the wooden structure was changed to iron.

Credit: flickr, ptrktn

The inner grounds of the Palace are closed to the public, except for the 2nd of January (New Year's Greeting), and the 23rd of December (the Emperor's Birthday). You can also join a 75 minutes tour that guides you around on imperial grounds if you make a reservation well ahead of time. The Imperial East Gardens are generally open to all visitors, besides Mondays, Fridays and special occasions. If you look around carefully, you can find old ruins of the Edo Castle here. Sannomaru Shozokan, Emperor Hirohito's (Emperor Showa) personal art collection is also in this garden exhibiting gorgeous kimonos and paintings. The moat next to Kitanomaru Park is Chidoriga-fuchi, which is another popular spot to observe the cherry blossoms. Heading south from here, you will see the giant building of the National Theatre in front of you, next to the Sakurada Moat, in case you feel like watching more noh, kabuki or kyogen (short, comic intermission between noh acts) performances.

Credit: flickr, Marufish

The Imperial Palace has been and is still effectively the very center of Tokyo as well as Japan. First the Edo Castle, then the Meiji Palace, then finally the National Diet Building and the Tokyo Station served this function. It is an ideal place for jogging and enjoying the rare greenery and fresh air in the middle of the metropolis.

Credit: Gergo Sastyin

Nippon Budokan

The Nippon Budokan, or Budokan in short, was originally built to house the judo competitions of the 1964 Tokyo Olympics. The designer Yamada Mamoru used the octagon shaped Yume-dono building of the Horyu-ji Temple (Nara Prefecture) as reference. The ridged lines of the main roof symbolize Mount Fuji. Since then it has been operating as a multi-functional venue for martial arts, combat sports and dance competitions, university entrance and graduation ceremonies, as well as for concerts. The first foreigner to perform at Budokan was the conductor Leopold Stokowski in 1965. He was followed by The Beatles in 1966, Led Zeppelin in 1971, Deep Purple in 1972 and 1973, Queen in 1975, just to mention a few of the legendary artists that graced its stage. If you do not mind sharing the experience with 10 thousand other fans, get tickets for the next gig!

Credit: Wikimedia, Wiiii

Yasukuni Shrine

Credit: Wikimedia, Lover of Romance

Easily accessible from Budokan: just cross the moat on the north and then turn left. Its predecessor was the Tokyo Shokon-sha from 1869 that changed its name to Yasukuni in 1879. Its main purpose was to comfort the spirits of the people, who sacrificed their honorable lives for the nation since 1853 in times of national crisis, such as the Japanese-Sino War, the Japanese-Russo War and the Pacific Theater of World War II. Currently about 2 and a half million spirits are enshrined here, including many war criminals.

Besides the two main events of Spring Festival (April 21-23) and Autumn Festival (Octorber 17-20), there is Hokyu-shiki on the 15th of August. This is the day when Emperor Showa announced their surrender in a live radio broadcast in 1945. As the name suggests, the highlight of the ceremony is when they set dozens of doves free.

If you want to know the exact time when cherry blossoms begin in Tokyo, look for the representative sakura tree near the shrine, which is used to pronounce the official opening of the hanami season by the Japan Meteorological Agency.

Other important sites include the statues of animals, the statue of a war widow with her children and that of a kamikaze pilot, as well as Yushukan, a museum that displays personal possessions, documents as well as weapons from World War II. Admission is between 9:00 and 16:30 costs 800 yen (500 yen for university students). The shrine gardens are generally open from 6:00 to 17:00 (or later, depending on the month).

Credit: flickr, Yasuyuki HIRATA

Jimbocho
This area towards the north of the Palace can be reached within 17 minutes on foot. Jimbocho has the highest density of books stores in all of Tokyo, especially when it comes to old, second-hand prints. They also have a big selection of English and photo/picture books.

Credit: flickr, hiroshi ataka

Kanda
Another 18 minutes walk north-east across the Sumida River will bring you to Kanda Myojin Shrine (or take the Shinjuku Metro Line to Awaji-cho, whence you walk straight north for about 12 minutes), the home of the famous Kanda Festival, which is considered to be one of the three

Credit: flickr, Marufish

largest traditional matsuris in Japan (the other two are Gion Festival in Kyoto and Tenjin Matsuri in Osaka). The extravagant version is held every other year (odd-numbered years) in mid-May, while the scale is considerably smaller in the years between. It is certainly an unforgettable sight to witness about 300 Edokkos (people who were born and raised in the Kanda area, the city center during the Edo Period) marching through the main streets carrying some 100 portable shrines on their shoulders. If you miss it, or you want to know more about the history of this festival, take a visit at the Kanda Myojin Museum (hours: 10:00-16:00, fee: 300 yen for adults).

Credit: Wikimedia, Kakidai

The shrine itself was originally built in 730 and even though it has been reconstructed and renovated several time since then, the current buildings are still able to provide you with an amazing atmosphere. Due to its proximity to Akihabara, it is frequently visited by people who need divine protection of their digital devices. You need not miss out either: take home a charm (omamori) to shield your gadgets from malicious forces (1,000 yen).

Yushima Seido, formerly Shoheizaka Academy, is also nearby, so why not take a look at the world's largest Confucius statue there?

On the way to Kanda Myojin or on the way back, visit the Holy Resurrection Cathedral (or Nikolai-do in Japanese), the main cathedral of the Japanese Orthodox Church. It was completed in 1891 and has survived both the Great Kanto Earthquake and the Great Tokyo Air Raid with only minor damages. If you go between 13:00 and 15:00, you

Credit: flickr, shibainu

can enter for a 300 yen admission fee.

Credit: flickr, Geoff Stearns

I am sure you feel hungry by now, so head back to Awaji-cho once again, where they have been serving the highest quality soba (buckwheat noodles) for more than a 100 years. Both of the following sell mainly "yabu" (rough) soba.

Kanda Yabu Soba
Address: Kanda Awaji-cho 2-10, Chiyoda-ku, Tokyo
Phone: +81-3-3251-0287
Hours: 11:30-21:00 (closed on Wednesdays)
Remarks: It was founded in 1880.

Kanda Matsuya
Address: Kanda Suda-cho 1-13, Chiyoda-ku, Tokyo
Phone: +81-3-3251-1556
Hours: 11:00-20:00 (Mon.-Fri.), 11:00-19:00 (Sat. and national holidays). Closed on Sundays.
Remarks: It was founded in 1884.

For an astonishing tea and Japanese confectionery experience, visit *Takemura*.

Takemura
Address: Kanda Suda-cho 1-19, Chiyoda-ku, Tokyo
Phone: +81-3-3251-2328
Hours: 11:00-20:00 (closed on Sundays and national holidays)
Remarks: It was founded in 1930.

Credit: Gergo Sastyin

Tokyo Station
The very center of Tokyo's, and as a matter of fact Japan's train network. A 21 minutes walk from Awaji-cho or a 3 minutes metro ride on the Marunouchi Metro Line (170 yen). The first plans were made in the end

of the 19th century, when an intermediate station became necessary to connect Ueno and Shimbashi stations. The fascinating red brick building was completed in 1914 and it currently has the largest number of platforms in Japan (9 train, 1 metro and 5 shinkansen platforms).

The station itself is full of intriguing historical elements. For example, on the platform of the 6th track (Yamanote Line, Tohoku Keihin Line towards Shinagawa Station) you can find a green, thick support pillar that has been here since the very beginning. After this, let's go to either the 4th or the 5th track platforms, from where we can observe a bronze post with a zero on the top of it. This particular piece was installed in 1969 and shows the beginning of the Yamanote Line.

Credit: Gergo Sastyin

By the way, did you know that two prime ministers have been assassinated at this station? One of them was Hara Takashi, who was stabbed by a station employee (from a different station) in 1921 (see the photo on the right), and the other one was Hamaguchi Osara, who was shot by a right wing group member in 1930 and died a year later from the infected wound.

Credit: flickr, fletcherjcm

Japan Rail Pass

You might want to consider buying a Japan Rail Pass that will allow you to travel freely on any JR trains, buses, most of the shinkansens (bullet trains) and one ferry line (JR-WEST Miyajima Ferry that runs between Miyajimaguchi, Hatsukaichi, Hiroshima and Miyajima-Itsukushima). On the condition that you are a temporary visitor with permanent foreign residency, you can order your pass before your visit and then pick it up in Japan.

There are two types of passes: the green for first-class cars, and the regular pass. Both passes are available for 7, 14 or 21 consecutive days starting on the first day of use, depending on your choice. Your best bet is probably the ordinary 21-day pass for 60 thousand yen, as 3 weeks is absolutely necessary if you want to travel around Japan and see most of the sites.

Roppongi

A few things about Roppongi

Credit: flickr, Antonio Fucito

You should learn a little bit about the history of Roppongi, before you head out with your friends to party all night long. Please? It used to be a land of samurai residences, later it was named Roppongi-cho, which was a monzen-machi (a neighborhood formed around a famous temple or shrine). Two main theories exist about the origins of the name "Roppongi", which literally means six trees. One of them attributes it to six pine trees that were planted around here. The other one sounds more compelling, as it interprets the name in an abstract fashion and connects it with the names of the six feudal lords, who had residences in this neighborhood and had a tree-related Chinese character in their names: Aoki, Hitotsuyanagi, Uesugi, Katagiri, Kutsuki and Takagi. Since the collapse of the Japanese bubble economy at the end of the 80's and the beginning of the so-called Lost Two Decades, the discos here have morphed into karaoke bars and kyabakuras. Kyabakura is a made-up word from cabaret and club, and they are similar to hostess bars, where you pay a certain amount per hour for a lady ("kyabakura-jo") to attend to you, serve you alcohol and keep you company. Currently Roppongi is home to many embassies (Spanish, Swedish, etc.), US military facilities, clubs, illegal casinos (gambling is prohibited in Japan, except for betting on a handful of sports), drug trafficking, organized crime and some foreign mafia. Nevertheless, it is still a very safe place in international standards, and, if you are careful, nothing could happen to you or your possessions.

How to get here? Take the Marunouchi Metro Line from Tokyo Station to Ginza Station, then change to the Hibiya Metro Line and get off at Roppongi Station.

Tokyo Midtown
First of all, let's go to Tokyo Midtown. It is connected underground with the station, so just follow the signs (5 minutes). It is basically like Sunshine City with shops, offices, mansions, a hotel, a hospital and a park. It was completed in 2007. The park area frequently becomes a venue for various lively events, such as gourmet or liquor nights, so check their schedule before you go.

Nogi Shrine
A 7-minute walk from Tokyo Midtown.
General Nogi Maresuke, an important figure in the Japanese-Russo war, and his wife, Shizuko are enshrined here. They committed suicide at their home on the day of Emperor Meiji's funeral (1912 September 13), as an atonement for all the lost lives (57,780 soldiers died or were wounded) in the Siege of Port Arthur. The shrine, standing very close to his original apartment, was built in 1923,

Credit: Wikimedia, Shika ryouse shomei

then rebuilt in 1983. The couple and both of their sons, who died during the war, are buried at the Aoyama Cemetery close-by (another 7 minutes walk). This was the first publicly owned cemetery, originally built in 1872. Hachiko, the famous dog I mentioned in the Shibuya chapter, also rests here with his beloved owner.

Roppongi Hills
Your next destination should be Roppongi Hills (12 minutes from Aoyama Cemetery or 15 minutes from Nogi Shrine). It is another complex similar to Tokyo Midtown, but much more impressive. It was opened in 2003 with the 54-story high Mori Tower in its center. The tower is quite enjoyable on its own:

Credit: Gergo Sastyin

On the 52nd floor you can find Mado Lounge, a hybrid of a cafe and an Italian restaurant. There is also an indoor observation deck (Tokyo City View) and the Mori Arts Center Gallery here. It has a spectacular view of the city both during the day and at night. Tokyo City view is open between 10:00 and 23:00 (Mon. – Thu., and on national holidays), or between 10:00 and 2:00 (Fri. – Sun., and the day before any national holiday). It costs 1,800 yen to enter (1,500 yen if you buy it beforehand at a convenience store; 1,200 yen for university students). From here you can also access the Sky Deck, which is an observation deck on the roof (the hours are 11:00-20:00, and the fee is an additional 500 yen). This floor is also the venue of occasional DJ events, large-scale Halloween parties, as well as the Roppongi Astronomy Club. This club holds star-gazing events and seminars/workshops on the 3rd Friday of every month. It is completely free to join them!

The 53rd floor houses the Mori Art Museum, which regularly holds exhibitions of contemporary art, photographs and architecture. It is open from 10:00 to 22:00 (Tuesdays 10:00-17:00) and costs 1,800 yen (1,200 yen for students). You are also allowed to enter Tokyo City View with the same ticket.

If you feel like reading something, visit the 49th floor, which has Academy Hills, a seminar / conference center with its own library.

Besides these, there are also several offices (TV Asahi, Lenovo Japan, J-WAVE commercial radio, GREE, etc.), and shops, of course. And this was only Mori Tower. Let's see what else Roppongi Hills has to offer:

Toho Cinemas Roppongi Hills is a rather luxurious cinema with reclining leather seats (Screen 7, +3,000 yen fee). I would recommend that you to go on the 1st or the 14th of the month, as a movie only costs 1,100 yen on these days. By the way, every weekend they have movies until 5:00 in the morning.

Mohri Garden, just outside the Hill Side restaurant and shopping area, is a 4,300 m² gorgeous garden with a lake, a waterfall, a river and many, many sakura and gingko trees. It is open every day between 7:00 and 23:00. Its extraordinary design, which began in 1650 lets you observe all fours seasons of Japan.

Credit: flickr, machu.

Credit: flickr, mhiguera

The Maman (French for "mother") spider is a bronze, stainless steel and marble sculpture by Louise Bourgeois at the base of Mori Tower. Look for the sac, which contains 26 marble eggs. You can also find a similar spider in Bilbao, Seoul, London and Ottawa. Its name comes from the fact that the artist dedicated this piece to her mother, Josephine.

After all this tiring sightseeing, it is time for a tsukemen (dip style ramen).

Tetsu
Address: Roppongi Hills North Tower B1F, Roppongi 6-2-31, Minato-ku, Tokyo
Phone: +81-3-3497-0154
Hours: 11:00-23:00

Clubs and other weird places
Get a can of *Ukon no chikara* (sort of tumeric mixed into a sugary drink) before the long night. It will likely save you from a bad hangover. Another rule about clubbing in Japan: you have to be at least 20 years old, so don't forget your ID!

Credit: Photozou, art_directter

You would think that Roppongi is stuffed with great dance clubs, however unfortunately this is not the case anymore. Most of them have closed, although I did manage to find one.

ELE TOKYO (formerly Warehouse)
It has two dance floors, the first one is a VIP area (reserve beforehand) and the basement is a regular one. The music depends on the night, and it varies from hip-hop, through trance to techno and house.
Address: Fukao Bldg. 1F/B1F, Azabujuban 1-4-5, Minato-ku, Tokyo
Phone: +81-3-5572-7535
Hours: 22:00-
Remarks: Free entry for ladies, and 3-4,000 yen for men, depending on the day.

And please, please forget about Gas Panic and Black Horse.

If you do not find *ELE TOKYO* satisfying, many people seem to recommend *ageHa* in Shin-Kiba or *Womb* in Shibuya. Even though the former is absolutely not in central Tokyo, there is a free shuttle bus every 15-30 minutes from Shibuya that will take you to *ageHa*, the biggest club in all of Japan. It consists of 3 dance floors, an outdoor swimming pool and an unbelievably large number of people.

ageHa
Address: Shin-Kiba 2-2-10, Koto-ku, Tokyo
Phone: +81-3-5534-2525
Hours: 23:00-5:00 (only open on Fridays and Saturdays)
Remarks: The admission fee can vary from 2,500 to 4,000 yen depending on the event.

Womb
Address: 1F, Maruyama-cho 2-16, Shibuya-ku, Tokyo
Phone: +81-3-5459-0039
Hours: 23:00-6:00
Remarks: It costs 2-4,000 yen to enter.

However, if you do decide to stay, you might as well explore Roppongi's bizarre selection of BDSM dungeons. For beginners, the soft S&M bar *Blackrose* is advisable. The thrill-seekers should head to *Jail* or *Mistress*...

Blackrose
Address: Yamanaka Kasumi-cho Bldg. 6F, Nishi-Azabu 3-24-19, Minato-ku, Tokyo
Phone: +81-3-3404-5556
Hours: 22:00-
Remarks: Funnily enough, this place is categorized as a wine bar on some websites.

Jail S&M and Fetish Bar
Address: Miyashita Blg. 2F, Roppongi 4-8-12, Minato-ku, Tokyo
Phone: +81-3-5772-5411
Hours: 19:00-4:00 (Mon. – Sat.), 19:00-23:00 (Sun. and national holidays)
Remarks: For men, it costs 5,000 yen / hour until midnight, or 5,000 yen until closing time after midnight (free drinks are included). For women, it costs 2,000 yen until closing time, regardless when they entered (free drinks are also included).

Roppongi Mistress Fetish Bar
Address: Daini Sanko Bldg. 3F, Roppongi 3-4-35, Minato-ku, Tokyo
Phone: +81-3-3585-5133
Hours: 20:00-1:00 (closed on Sun. and national holidays)
Remarks: For men, it costs 10,000 yen / hour (only the first drink is included). For women, it is only 1,000 until closing time. For couples, it is 12,000 yen until midnight and 6,000 yen / 30 minutes after midnight.

After a long night of dancing or being whipped, you should get some drunchies (drunk munchies) at a kebab restaurant such as *Deniz Kebab*.

Deniz Kebab
Address: Kita-AzabuBldg. 1-2F, Roppongi 3-13-10, Minato-ku, Tokyo
Phone: +81-3-6804-2941
Hours: 24/7

Just pick up a wrap and walk towards Tokyo Tower on the Gaien Higashi-dori. It takes 20 minutes on foot to get there, but it is utterly gorgeous at sunrise. Of course, it is also beautiful at night, which you have probably already confirmed yourself from Roppongi Hills. Tokyo Tower, the 333 meters tall structure was built in 1958 and since then has become one of the symbols of the capital.

Credit: Gergo Sastyin

If you still have enough stamina in you to continue (sleep is for the weak!), catch the Hibiya Line metro at the Kamiya-cho Station until Kasumigaseki, then change to Chiyoda Metro Line until you reach Akasaka Station. It should not take you more than 21 minutes. Have a cup of espresso and a snack at the extremely cute *TBS Boobo Café*, inside the Akasaka Sacas TBS building, and recharge for the next day.

TBS Boobo Café
Address: TBS Hoso Bldg. 1F, Akasaka 5-3-6, Minato-ku, Tokyo
Phone: +81-3-5571-4021
Hours: 10:00-18:30

Credit: Wikimedia, Wiiii

While you are here, you should visit the Akasaka Palace, one of the two State Guesthouses of the Japanese government. It was originally designed to serve as the Imperial Palace for the Crown Prince, when it was built in 1909. You need to apply in advance to gain admission, but trust me it is worth it.

On the way back to the station, jump in for a late afternoon concert at Akasaka Blitz, then finish the day with a dinner at *Ninja Akasaka*, where the staff is (obviously) dressed in ninja outfits and perform various ninja tricks for you if you are lucky.

Ninja Akasaka
Address: Akasaka Tokyu Plaza 1F, Nagata-cho 2-14-3, Chiyoda-ku, Tokyo
Phone: +81-3-5157-3936
Hours: 17:00-1:00 (Mon. – Sat.), 17:00-23:00 (Sun. and national holidays)

Tokyo Bay

This is our last area in Tokyo, although technically some parts belong to Chiba Prefecture. As it is quite large, it might take 2-3 days to cover everything, especially if you are planning to visit the Tokyo Disney Resort and other theme parks.

Shinagawa

Credit: Wikimedia, Kure

Walking here from Akasaka or Roppongi might be too rough, so I recommend you take the Chiyoda Metro Line from Akasaka until Hibiya, then change to JR Keihin Tohoku Line at the Yuraku-cho Station (21 minutes, 330). It is one of the biggest hubs of the Japanese railway system that connects Tokyo with Northern, Southern and Western Japan, as well as with Narita and Haneda airports. It started operating in 1872 and immediately became part of the Shimbashi-Yokohama line. In 2002, they installed a monument on the platform of the 5th and the 6th tracks celebrating the 130th year of their opening. This station will have a central function in rearranging the metropolitan infrastructure to prepare for the 2020 Tokyo Olympics. This is also the station, whence a state-of-the-art maglev train, Chuo Shinkansen will connect Tokyo with Nagoya (by 2027, 40 minutes) and Osaka (by 2045, 67 minutes). The technology will allow the train to reach a 505 km/hour speed (during testing, it reached 603 km/hour, which made it the fastest train in the world).

Just outside the station, have a bowl of ramen on Shinatatsu Ramen Street or a hamburger at *T. G.I. Friday's*, then head to Mita Station via Keikyuu Main Line / Asakusa Metro Line (they are virtually the

Credit: flickr, Guilhem Vellut

same line, so you do not need to change anywhere).

Keio University Mita Campus

Credit: Wikimedia

Five minutes from the station you will find yourself at Keio University, the most prestigious and highest ranking private university in Japan. It was founded in 1858 as a Rangakujuku (a private school, where Japanese people could learn Western academics). Moreover, the founder was Fukuzawa Yukichi, a liberal ideologist, writer and teacher, who was truly one of the most influential figures in modern Japanese history. And yes, he is the man on the 10 thousand yen banknote. He was the Benjamin Franklin, the Voltaire, and the Mustafa Kemal Atatürk of Japan.

Why is this campus worth a visit? Here you can see the first auditorium of Japan, the Mita Auditorium, which was built in 1875 and founded entirely by Fukuzawa's own money. Although the original design was influenced by western architecture, it also exhibits the typical Japanese tile-roofed wooden structure and Namako walls (white grid pattern on black slate). Fukuzawa believed that public speech and debate were extremely important, thus he was the one who translated and introduced these concepts to Japan for the first time. You must not miss the historical library building either (see the photo on the right). It was built in 1907 to honor the 30th anniversary of the university. Its gothic appearance, along with its red brick and granite material makes it a truly impressive structure. On school days, the building is open between 8:45 and 21:50 (weekdays) or 8:45 and 17:50 (Saturdays).

Credit: Photozou, Rubber Soul

Shimbashi

Credit: flickr, Stéfan

A 37-minute walk along the bay or a 4-minute ride on the Asakusa Metro Line (180 yen) from Keio University. It is the ultimate salarymen paradise, as it is equipped with an abudance of offices and gado-shita style small bars (just like in Yuraku-cho). The Shimbashi Station was the first train station in the history of Japan, connecting Tokyo with Yokohama since 1872. You should visit the Railway History Exhibition Hall that holds many artifacts and photographs related to the history of this area, where the first trains were running. It is open between 10:00 and 17:00 (closed on Mondays), and it is free to enter.

The first gay bar after World War II, "Yanagi" was opened here, serving such famous customers as Alain Delon, Yves Saint-Laurent and Pierre Cardin. Unfortunately it closed in 1989, although currently there are 74 related locations in this area to choose from, making Shimbashi the 3rd biggest gay district in Tokyo (after Shinjuku, and Ueno/Asakusa). Among these, *Town House Tokyo* should definitely be highlighted, although you should expect a more mature atmosphere here compared to the Shinjuku LGBT scene.

Town House Tokyo
Address: Cortile Ginza Bldg. 6F, Shimbashi 1-11-5, Minato-ku, Tokyo
Phone: +81-3-3289-8558
Hours: 18:00-2:00 (weekdays), 16:00-0:00 (Sat.), closed on Sun. and national holidays
Remarks: It has karaoke (free on weekends), cheap drinks, and regular underwear-only nights.

For the ladies, regrettably there are not very many options around here, as most of the women-only bars seem to cluster around Shinjuku 2-chome. The most popular amongst these are *Kinswomyn* and *Motel #203*.

Kinswomyn
Address: Daiichi Tenka Bldg. 3F, Shinjuku 2-15-10, Shinjuku-ku, Tokyo
Phone: +81-3-3354-8720
Hours: 20:00-4:00 (closed on Tue.)

Motel #203
Adress: Sunny Corpo 203, Shinjuku 2-7-2, Shinjuku-ku, Tokyo
Phone: +81-3 6383 4649
Hours: 20:00-4:00 (Mon. – Sat.), 20:00-2:00 (Sun.), closed on Tue.
Remarks: On Thursdays, men can enter as well.

Tokyo Disney Resort

Credit: flickr, f59t8y

From Shimbashi, take the JR Keihin Tohoku Line to Yuraku-cho, walk to Tokyo Station, then get on the JR Keiyo Line to Maihama.

Tokyo Disney Resort is composed of two theme parks, Tokyo Disneyland and Tokyo DisneySea. It is the first Disney amusement park that was opened outside of the USA, in 1983. DisneySea was only added later, in 2001.

Tokyo Disneyland has the 2nd largest number of visitors in a year (within amusement parks / theme parks) after the Magic Kingdom in Florida. It is made up of seven themed lands. Try their jalapeno & cheese popcorn!

Tokyo DisneySea is the first Disney park with a water/sea theme. Originally this park was supposed to be built at Long Beach (Los Angeles), but the local municipality did not agree to the plans. Like Tokyo Disneyland, this park also has seven themed ports. It targets a more mature audience by serving alcohol and offering gourmet menus. An absolute recommendation is *Ristorante Di Canaletto* in the Mediterranean Harbor. It is not only aesthetically pleasing from outside or inside, but if you sit on the terrace, you can enjoy the view of sliding gondolas in the canal in front of you. As if you were in Venice!

Credit: Gergo Sastyin

There are a plenty of reliable websites that can help you plan your trip to the last details, but I can give you a few pieces of information. There is no single ticket for both of the parks, so you need to buy them individually. The actual price will depend on whether you go at daytime or only in the evening. I do recommend DisneySea over Disneyland, as it is indeed a unique experience you cannot find elsewhere.

Odaiba

Back to Shimbashi, from where you should take the Yurikamome Line, a monorail service that provides you with an amazing view on Tokyo Bay and many sites on the way, such as the Rainbow Bridge, Tokyo Tower, Tokyo Skytree, and Tokyo Gate Bridge. There will be several bold architectural pieces as well: the Fuji TV Building, the Telecom Center and the Tokyo Big Sight (see the photo on the left). The last one is also known as Tokyo International Exhibition Center, and is home to the Tokyo

Credit: flickr, Dick Thomas Johnson

97

International Anime Fair, the Comiket Comic Fair and the Tokyo Motor Show.

What is Odaiba exactly? It literally means fort, which is not a coincidence. After Commodore Perry came to Japan to negotiate a trade agreement in 1853, the government decided to build 11 forts near the shore with cannons. These were called Shinagawa-Daiba or Odaiba. In the end, none of them were used and Japan peacefully opened its harbors to the West. Much later on, the bay saw the creation of a dozen artificial lands as an attempt to expand the metropolis. The Eastern part of the 13th was named Odaiba, as a memento of the historical forts, of which the 3rd and the 6th still exist nearby.

Get off at Odaiba Kaihin-koen Station for Decks Tokyo Beach, where you can get lost among the over 3 million Lego bricks, in virtual-reality games or in the gorgeous view of the Tokyo Bay.

Legoland Discovery Center
Hours: 10:00-20:00 (weekdays), 10:00-21:00 (weekends and national holidays)
Fee: 1,500-2,200 yen, depending on the time and whether you buy it there or online

Sega Joypolis
Hours: 10:00-20:00
Fee: 2,400-3,900 yen for adults (1,900-2,900 yen for children), depending on your time of visit

Credit: Gergo Sastyin

The Odaiba Statue of Liberty, a replica of the French sculpture, was installed near the Odaiba Seaside Park (Kaihin-koen) in 2000, due to popular demand since the French original stood here for a year in 1998-1999 in commemoration of the "French Year in Japan".

From here you can walk directly to Aqua City Odaiba, where you should sit in at *Kua'aina* for a perfect Hawaiian burger. DiverCity Tokyo Plaza with its life-sized Gundam robot is also just a few steps away.

Credit: flickr, karitsu

Kua'aina
Address: Aqua City Odaiba 4F, Daiba 1-7-1, Minato-ku, Tokyo
Phone: +81-3-3599-2800
Hours: 11:00-23:00

Credit: Wikimedia, Rs1421

Walk south along the Yurikamome Line for 11 minutes to reach the Museum of Maritime Science. It is easy to notice, as the main building looks like a giant cruiseship. If you are a water person, you will love it. They are open from 10:00 until 17:00 and the admission is free of charge.

14 more minutes along the rails and you will be at Telecom Center Station, where you can finally relax at Oedo Onsen Monogatari, a hot spring theme park that makes you feel like you traveled back in time to the Edo Period. It costs 1,980 yen to enter after 18:00 and an additional 2,000 yen for the overnight stay.

Cruise on the Sumida River
The next morning take the Yurikamome Line back to Hinode Station, where you can change to the Tokyo Water Bus. For only 720 yen, off you go to Asakusa on the Sumida River (40 minutes). Otsukare sama, you have explored most of Tokyo!

Credit: flickr, Tatsuo Yamashita

Yokohama

Yokohama, about 30-40 km south of Tokyo, is the second most populated city in Japan with 3.7 million people. It has been functioning as one of the main harbors of Japan, and it also used to be the center of international trade and transportation for several decades after it was forced to open to the world in 1859. It is a popular place to visit for Tokyo citizens as well, due to its intriguing history and proximity to the sea.

First of all you should get to Yokohama Chinatown as early as possible. From Asakusa, you need to take the Asakusa Metro Line, which will turn into Keikyu Main Line after 11 stations, until Yokohama Station. Here you have to change to the Minatomirai Line, then get off at Motomachi-Chukagai Station. The entire trip takes 54 minutes and costs 790 yen.

Yokohama Chinatown
One of the three Chinatowns that can be found in Japan (the others are in Kobe and Nagasaki). This is considered to be the largest Chinatown in Japan, and in Asia for that matter, with over 500 shops for an area as small as 0.2 km². It dates all the way back to 1855 and there are currently more than 6,000 Chinese citizens living here. If you happen to be here in February, make sure you visit the neighborhood during the Chinese New Year celebrations. They usually have parades and traditional Chinese performances with lion and dragon heads.

Credit: flickr, geraldford

In order to enter, you need to pass through one of the four main gates of the district. Inside, you will find five more gates and the colorful temple of Kanteibyo (or Kuan Ti Miao), which was built in 1873 to honor Kuan Ti, the god of fortune and flourishing business. Definitely try the street food here. Ramen noodles, dumplings, steamed buns... *Kocho* allegedly has the best steamed buns ("nikuman" in Japanese) in the world, so I figure you should give it a try.

Kocho
Address: Yamashita-cho 138-24, Naka-ku, Yokohama-shi
Phone: +81-50-5797-1106
Hours: 11:00-22:00

Find a tapioca seller, and keep walking around while sipping on it. You will realize that people watching in Yokohama Chinatown can be quite a fun activity on its own.

Motomachi

After Chinatown, you should walk south to reach the old foreign district of Motomachi. Once again, February would be a perfect time to be here, as they annually hold a large-scale sale on the Motomachi Shopping Street, called "Charming Sale". If you are not interested in shopping, make your way towards the Yokohama Foreign General Cemetery, where you can actually enter a small section with approximately 4,200 graves in it. It is only open to the public on weekends and national holidays, in exchange for a 200-300 yen donation. Get lost on the hills of Motomachi and you might be able to discover some historical western-style houses.

Credit: Photozou, matsukaz

Minatomirai

Let's take the Minatomirai Line again, this time backwards. Get off at the Minatomirai Station, which is located within the district of Minato Mirai 21. The name, chosen from submissions from the public in 1981, reflects the efforts of the locals to make Yokohama a "harbor city of the future 21st century". There are many things to see here, so let's look at them one by one.

Yokohama Landmark Tower is a shopping, hotel and office complex completed in 1993, which used to be Japan's tallest skyscraper until 2014 (now it is Abeno Harukas). Go up to the Sky Garden on the 69th floor with Japan's fastest elevator (750 m/min), where you can enjoy the beautiful view of Yokohama. It is open from 10:00 to 21:00, and the admission fee is 1,000 yen.

Credit: Gergo Sastyin

In front of Landmark Tower, you will see the Nippon Maru sailboat as part of the Nippon Maru Memorial Park. The boat was built in 1930 and its main function was to train sailors. During the approximately 54 years of its activity, it traveled 45.4 times the Earth's circumference and raised 11,500 sailors. Imagine you are one of these sailors, and explore each floor and corner of the ship (10:00-17:00, 600 yen)!

Credit: Gergo Sastyin

The Yokohama Cosmo World amusement park was originally built for the Yokohama Exotic Showcase (YES in short) '89, but it has continued to operate since. Cross the water to the artificial island, where the Cosmo Clock 21 stands, the biggest digital clock (Citizen, of course) embedded Ferris wheel in the world. For 800 yen, you can observe the

Credit: Gergo Sastyin

102

entire bay area including the Landmark Tower. The ride takes about 15 minutes.

Credit: Gergo Sastyin

If you walk to the other side of the island, the Yokohama Red Brick Warehouse will appear in front of you. The two sections were built as customs buildings in the beginning of the 20th century. Currently, various events and exhibitions are organized inside and outside.

Are you here in August? Don't miss the Kanagawa Shimbun Fireworks Festival, which is best watched from the nearby Osanbashi Pier with a beer in your hand.

When it is nearing late afternoon, walk back towards Cosmo Clock 21, until you reach Yokohama World Porters. Here choose from one of the restaurants that look on the water, you won't regret it. After enjoying your dinner at sunset, the most stunning view on the area is offered

Credit: Gergo Sastyin

by the Yamashita Park, which is only a 14 minutes walk away. Absolutely breathtaking, isn't it? While you're there, take a look at the Girl Scout Statue and the Hikawa Maru ocean liner from 1929.

At the end of the day, how about staying in a hotel that looks at Minatomirai 21? Navios Yokohama, which is right on the artificial island, offers plenty of rooms like that for 6-10 thousand yen a night. Just don't forget to reserve ahead on Jalan.net.

Southern Yokohama

Credit: Wikimedia, Urashimataro

The next morning hop on the number 8 or 58 bus at Honmachi 4-chome, just across the water to the south. It will take you to Sankei-en Garden in 38-39 minutes. This traditional Japanese-style garden was designed by Hara Sankei (real name Hara Tomitaro), a wealthy businessman trading silk, and opened in 1906. Have a cup of tea surrounded by historical feudal lord residences, ponds and a three-story pagoda (9:00-17:00, 500 yen).

From Sannotani, catch bus number 101 or 54 to the Negishi Station, where you need to get on the JR Negishi Line until Shinsugita. Here you change to Seaside Line and ride the train until Hakkeijima (69 minutes and 690 yen in total). Hakkeijima Sea Paradise opened in 1993 and consists mainly of an aquarium, Aqua Resorts and an amusement park, Pleasure Land. By the way, Japan seems to have the highest number of aquaria in the world (somewhere between 60 and 70, depending on the source). The most popular attractions of the Aqua Resorts are the whale sharks (the only ones on display in Eastern Japan) and the "touch and learn lagoon", where you are allowed to have direct contact with dolphins, penguins and other species (4,550-5,050 yen, depending on the season). At Pleasure Land, make sure to try Japan's first surf coaster that runs partly above water (1000 yen for a ride)! Check the opening hours before you go. You should also keep in mind that if you want to fully enjoy

Credit: Wikimedia, Daddy t3

Hakkeijima Sea Paradise, it might be advisable to set aside an extra day here.

Credit: Wikimedia, 小池 隆

Once you are done splashing around, grab a lunch box somewhere near the station and take the Seaside Line back to Umino-koen Shibakuchi. From here, walk northwest for about 11 minutes to the Shomyo-ji Temple, which belongs to the Shingon Risshu Buddhist sect and was built around 1258. The utterly peaceful garden was added in 1320 and later reproduced in 1987. The colors, the silence, and the slightly overwhelming feeling of history can make it a perfect location for lunch. It is open between 8:30 and 16:30 for no admission fee at all.

I hope you are up for a swim (if the season and the weather permits, naturally), because you are going to Zushi, which is right at one of Eastern Japan's most popular beaches. Apparently, however, tattoos are prohibited since 2014, so hide them well. Get on a Keikyu Main Line train at Kanazawa Bunko and in 10 minutes you will be at Zushi.

Credit: Gergo Sastyin

From the station, it is only a 17 minutes walk to the beach or a 4 minutes bus ride (number 11). Enjoy!

Kamakura

Kamakura
One of Japan's most important religious centers with more than 70 active temples and shrines. Most of them are open daily 9:00-16:00 for 100-300 yen entrance fee. Kamakura used to be the capital during the Kamakura Period (1185-1333). In modern times, it has been the home of many influential writers and artists, who are called Kamakura-bunshi, such as Akutagawa Ryunosuke and Kawabata Yasunori.

Credit: Gergo Sastyin

Kamakura is part of the Shonan area, which basically includes the entire shore of Sugami Bay, between the Izu and Miura peninsulas. Its name, apparently, comes from a former similarity between the medieval Chinese prefecture, Hunan and Kamakura, precisely that both of them were/are the mecca of Zen buddhism within their own country. Shonan has a fun and relaxing atmosphere, something similar to California, although with more nature and history. Besides swimming and chilling, you can also try clam digging (shiohigari), surfing (both summer and winter) or windsurfing. Just be careful, the beach is reserved in late August every year by the jellyfish community.

Take the JR Yokosuka Line from Zushi to Kita-Kamakura Station (7 minutes, 170 yen), or the JR Shonan-Shinjuku Line (9 minutes, 170 yen).

Temples and Shrines
Walk east from the station to Engaku-ji, which was built in 1282 and to this day still houses priests practicing and studying Zen here. Even the public can join their zazen

Credit: Wikimedia, Tarourashima

(meditation) sessions on the weekends. It is known for its traditional gardens and gigantic bell from 1301.

Credit: flickr, Nao Kitano

Cross to the other side of the rails, where you will find narrow stone stairs in a cedar forest leading up to the Jochi-ji Temple. It is part of the same branch of Buddhism as Engaku-ji, and was built a year later, in 1283. Look for the Nectar Well (Kanrono-ido), which is one of the ten fresh water sources in Kamakura, as well as the three wooden statues of the past, present and future Buddhas.

Crossing the rails again towards south-east, you will reach a big green area with Kencho-ji Temple in it, which dates back to 1253. It is the oldest Zen related building in Kamakura and certainly worth a visit, especially for the colorful decoration of Dharma Hall (Hatto) and the beautiful dragon painting on its ceiling. From here you can take the Tenen Hiking Trail that leads up to Zuisen-ji through forests and hills in about 60-90 minutes. The Zen rock garden here with its flowers and plum trees should not be missed.

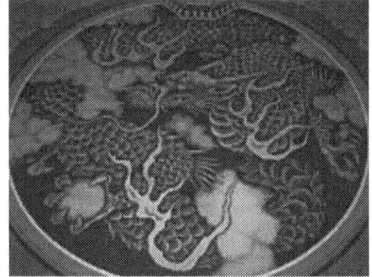

Credit: Wikimedia, Urashimataro

After Zuisenji, walk west to Tsurugaoka Hachiman-gu Shrine, one of the highlights of Kamakura. It was founded in 1083 and moved to its current location by Minamoto Yoritomo, the first shogun of the Kamakura government, in 1180.The shrine is dedicated to Hachiman, the protecting deity of the Minamoto clan. Personally,

Credit: flickr, d'n'c

107

my favorite part is the lotus pond with the Taiko (drum) Bridge over it. The pond separates into two sections, the Minamoto side and the Taira (the Minamoto clan's arch enemy) side. The former has three tiny islands, which implies "birth", "prosperity" or "creation" (same pronunciation as the number three) and the latter has four of them, referring to "death" (again, same as number four in Japanese).

If you have time for another brief visit, go to Hokokuji Temple, towards the southeast across the Shakuji River. It is also called the Bamboo Temple due to its abundant bamboo groves growing inside the garden.

Walk back to Kamakura Station, then walk southwest towards Hase Station (23 minutes) or take the Enoshima Dentetsu Line there (Enoden, in short; 6 minutes, 190 yen). In the early 40's, it is said that the train used to be so crowded that the window glasses would break and 10 passangers would have to sit inside the toilet to fit into the car. Enoden is by far my favorite train line in Japan, as the view is always unbelievable and the cars are painted happy colors (green or purple). Head north from the station and order a lunch set at *Shamoji*. Try their shirasu (small anchovies or sardines)!

Credit: Photozou, Rubber Soul

Shamoji
Address: Hase 1-15-2, Kamakura-shi
Phone: +81-4-6724-5888
Hours: 12:00-15:00 (lunch), 18:00-21:00 (dinner)

Hurry up, you do not have that much time left before the temples close. Go north towards Kotoku-in, where you can find one of the two most important Buddha statues in Japan. There used to be three of them (in Kyoto, then in Kobe), but the third one was always destroyed one way or another. The other statue is at Todaiji in Nara, by the way, which I also highly recommend you visit one day. Both the temple and the 11-meter tall statue are surrounded by mystery and several different theories exist regarding their history. What we know, however, is that if you pay an extra 20 yen, you can see the Buddha from the inside.

Credit: Gergo Sastyin

The next destination will be the last temple for today, unless you would like to walk around a bit more, later. Hasedera, built in 736 according to the legends, is just a few minutes away from the Hase Station. It is famous for an almost 10-meter tall wooden statue of the eleven-faced Kannon, the goddess of mercy, as it is considered to be one of the largest of its kind. Strangely enough, ten out of eleven heads are quite small and they casually stand on top of the main, bigger head. On the way up to the Kannon-do Hall, where the aforementioned sculpture is enshrined, you should peek into Jizo-do as well. It contains hundreds of small jizo statues, the patrons of travelers and deceased children. They are easily recognizable from their adorable faces and occasional red bibs. Visit the observation deck nearby and enjoy the view while munching on a dango (rice dumplings on a stick with sugar and soy sauce). On the

Credit: flickr, Brian Sterling

way back, take a break in the temple garden at the base of the slope, where you should see the Benten statue (do you remember the chapter about Ueno?) that was allegedly carved by Kukai himself, the priest who founded the Shingon school of Buddhism.

Before leaving Hase behind, I would recommend looking around in the local souvenir and handcrafts stores, which are great sources of ceramics and washi (Japanese-style paper).

Enoshima

Jump on the next Enoden to Enoshima (19 minutes, 270 yen). This land-tied island is currently inhabited by about 360 citizens and has two caves (Iwaya Caves) as well as steep cliffs on the southern side. The stone plates below offer a perfect location for sunbathing and fishing during low tide. You can also climb the hill to the giant bell, where couples attach a lock with their names on it onto the fence, after ringing the bell together. This tradition comes from a legend about a love story involving Benten goddess and a reckless five-headed dragon. If you have 10 thousand yen in your pocket, rent a room in the local ryokan, Iwamotoro. Otherwise, you can find cheaper options near the Kamakura Station for sure. If you decide to stay for the night and the next day falls on a weekend or a national holiday, take a boat back to the mainland in the morning. Oh, and don't forget to bring your camera. Enoshima offers an excellent view of Mount Fuji, which just so happens to be your next destination!

Credit: pixabay, yuzu

Mount Fuji

The Symbol of Japan

Credit: flickr, hoge asdf

No guidebook about Japan or Tokyo can be complete without mentioning Mount Fuji, which is not only the highest point on the Japanese islands, but also the most magnificent view in the entire country. Its imposing presence is mainly due to the year-round snow-capped peak that reaches an impressive 3,776 meters and the gradual inclines that seem like they never end, as well as the fact that it is visible from 20 of the 47 prefectures of Japan, from an approximately 300 km radius. In 2014 they finally succeeded in taking a photograph all the way from Kyoto! So nobody should wonder why this mountain is so important for the Japanese.

It is an active stratovolcano that erupted in 1707-8 for the last time. Since the capital moved to Edo in the 17th century, the volcanic cone has been the theme of countless paintings, such as Hokusai's *36 Views of Mount Fuji* and Utagawa Hiroshige's work with the same title. Many works of literature have depicted the mountain as well, including the remarkable Manyoshu, which is the oldest collection of Japanese poetry. It is told that the first person to ascend was an En no Ozunu, a mystic and ascetic, in 663, and the first foreigner was Sir Rutherford Alcock in 1868. In 1872, they lifted the ban that prevented women from entering this sacred territory. Nowadays it is a popular touristic location for both Japanese and foreign tourists.

Credit: flickr, Go Uryu

Climbing Mount Fuji

Credit: Gergo Sastyin

The climbing trails are usually open only between early July and mid-September. You should be well prepared and carry rain and cold protection, a headlamp and a map, at least. Water, snacks, and trekking boots are also recommended. These are all necessary to help you cope with temperature change (more than 20 celsius degrees difference compared to the foothills), thunder, lightning and dense fog. To avoid mountain sickness, you should drink water frequently, rest at regular intervals at locations such as mountain huts, walk slowly at a constant pace and breathe deeply. All the four trails are color-coded, so make sure to follow your path at the junctions.

The yellow Yoshida Trail starts at 2,300 meters and has zigzag paths (up to the 7th station) as well as slightly rocky ones (5-7 hours for ascent, 3-5 hours for descent). The red Subashiri trail starts at 2,000 meters, has a relatively mild and is tree-covered (up to the 7th station; 5-8 hours for ascent, 3-5 hours for descent). The green Gotemba Trail begins at 1,450 meters with a gentle slope and lots of volcanic gravel (until the 8th station; 7-10 hours for ascent, 3-6 hours for descent). The blue Fujinomiya trail has the highest altitude at starting point (2,400 m), and it is generally quite steep and rocky (4-7 hours for ascent, 2-4 hours for descent). The Yoshida and the Fujinomiya trails are the most popular ones, because they have sufficient number of mountain huts,

Credit: Photozou, Tom1

especially on the way up, and first-aid centers. The 10th station denotes the summit for all trails. If you do decide to hike up, definitely avoid going during Obon week (mid-August), because this is the busiest time every year. If you are experienced enough, you should try to go in early July or early September, when there are less student groups, although the weather can be somewhat unpredictable.

Credit: flickr, Hajime NAKANO

If you ask me, I suggest you climb up until the 7th or 8th station on the first day, take a few hours sleep in one of the mountain huts, then continue to the summit early morning to see the sunrise. (Don't forget that the sun rises between 4:30 and 5:00 during summer!) Walk around the crater – this should take you about an hour – then descend.

The Yoshida Trail has the largest number of mountain huts, and it usually costs 5,000 yen for a night per person (7,000 yen with meal), although some huts allow you to stay on a per hour basis (1-2,000 yen). Bring some cash with you even if you do not plan to stay in a hut, as the toilets are generally not free either. Moreover, they will ask for a 1,000 yen donation at the head of each trail (5th station).

There are many ways to get to the trails, thus you should look into the transportation options after you have decided which trail to take and when. Have a nice climb!

Credit: flickr, Nicky Pallas

Top 6 Famous Festivals in Japan

There are two main types of festivals in Japan: nationwide festivals and local festivals. While nationwide festivals do, of course, share some invariable features, they can also differ quite a bit depending on the region. And, similarly, even though the local celebrations are quite unique to that specific area, many of them also have a fair number of characteristics in common.

 A characteristic seen in many local festivals is the carrying of the kami (deity) of the regional shrine around the town/neighborhood in mikoshis (palanquins, portable shrines), along with many decorated daishis/yatais (floats), on or around which you can normally see volunteers playing various instruments.

 These festivals are also great opportunities to wear traditional clothes such as kimonos or yukatas (summer kimonos), zori straw sandals and tabi socks, as well as eat cheap (but good!) Japanese street food and blend in with the locals.

Nationwide Festivals

Seijinshiki / Coming of Age Day *(2nd Monday of January)*
Its roots date back to ancient times, when it was something of an initiation ceremony.

The current celebration is based on a youth festival organized in Saitama Prefecture in 1946, and aims to instill hope and a bright outlook on the next generation, who will have the central role in forming the future of Japan.

It is generally held every year on the 2nd Monday of January, although some neighborhoods prefer to hold it during the Obon Festival (see below), as the local youth is more likely to have returned home during that holiday. To be celebrated, a person must have celebrated his/her 20th birthday between last April and the April following.

Hinamatsuri / Doll Festival *(March 3rd)*

Dolls wearing Heian Period dresses are displayed along with peach flowers, while sushi and shirozake (sweet sake) are consumed.

Originally, the dolls served as toys for the daughters of aristocrat parents in the Heian Period, however over time, it became part of the gosekku (five annual celebrations; four of them are between seasons, and one is between years).

Hanami *(March-April, depending on the region)*

It literally means "flower viewing" and is by far the most magical season in Japan (the second one would be momiji, the season of autumn leaves; see below).

During hanami, practically everyone goes to one of the parks with cherry trees (or "sakura" in Japanese) and enjoys the stunning view along with food and lots of alcohol. In fact, most of the time they are more interested in the consumption part, rather than in the flower viewing itself.

There is even a Japanese proverb, "Hana yori dango" (rice dumplings over flowers) that expresses this sentiment.

Tanabata / Star Festival *(July 7th or August 6th-8th; the latter is closer to the original date of the lunar calendar)*

It is also one of the gosekku, and used to be a part of Obon, however due to the introduction of the western calendar, it became independent. Nowadays it is spent attaching wishes in the form of tanzakus (colorful papers) to bamboo branches.

This tradition comes from a Chinese myth, in which the lovers, Cowherd Star (Altair) and Weaver Star (Vega) are separated by the Milky Way and only allowed to meet once every year, on this very day. Therefore it is not very surprising that besides Japan, it is also celebrated in China, Taiwan, Korea and Vietnam.

The most famous festival is held in Sendai, where the streets are covered in splendid hand-made streamers and other smaller paper decorations.

Obon *(July 13th-16th or August 13th-16th depending on the area)*

This is one of the most important Japanese traditions, when families get together to welcome the spirits of their ancestors.

They usually place various food offerings in front of the butsudan (Buddhist altar), visit and clean the family's graves. Toro nagashi, or floating lanterns marks the end of Obon in many regions, when people set a lit lantern afloat onto a river or a sea, as they believe that these lights will guide the spirits back to their world.

Another characteristic of Obon is the bon odori, a dancing event on the last night, which everyone is welcome to join and which takes place inside the gardens of shrines/temples or even near stations.

Momiji-gari *(September-December, depending on the region)*

You can surely say that in Japan every season has its own personality. Spring has sakura, summer has loud cicadas and tsuyu (rainy season between May and July), autumn has momiji (autumn leaves) and taiphoons, and winter has snow and Japanese apricots.

In autumn, it is absolutely recommended to visit one of the famous momiji observation places such as the Oirase Stream in Aomori Prefecture, Nikko in Tochigi Prefecture or basically any shrine and temple in Kyoto City. The "-gari" (literally "hunting") ending refers to the way Japanese people used to break off the branches and observe the leaves from the top of their palms. Luckily it is not a habit anymore.

Shichi-Go-San *(November 15th)*

The name of this celebration literally means 7-5-3. On this day, parents visit their local shrines/temples to pray for the health and happiness of their 3, 5 or 7 years old child(ren) (this celebration follows the traditional East-Asian age reckoning, in which newborns start at the age of 1) . Originally it was only performed in the Kanto area, however it has recently spread to the entire country.

Besides the prayers, there used to be three rituals to be carried out, which were specific to the gender and the age of the child: at age 3, the girls could grow out their hair again (until that both the boys' and the girls' heads had to be shaved); at age 5, the boys could wear hakama pants; at age 7, the girls could wear the same obi belt as the adults.

Nowadays these rituals can be performed regardless of gender and since shaving the children's heads is not a custom anymore, it has been replaced with an adapted version of the tradition. In the past, people used to shave the heads of their children, believing that this would enable the children to have stronger and healthier hair.

The modernized version of this is that at age 3, both genders receive their first haircut. The result is photographed and kept safe in every Japanese family's photo album.

Omisoka, New Year's Eve *(December 31)*

Before you can get rid of all the 108 wordly desires (bonno) by listening to the temple bells at midnight, you need to clean your house thoroughly (called osoji) and pay off your debts!

You should also eat toshigoshi-soba, which guarantees that your good luck will be extended, just like your noodles.

Shogatsu, New Year *(January 1st-3rd, 1st-7th or 1st-15th depending on the region)*

Shogatsu is supposed to signify all of January (as the word *gatsu* means month), however it is generally used to refer to either sanganichi (1-3) or matsu-no-uchi (1-7 or 1-15).

It is customary to visit your relatives, co-workers and friends during shogatsu (onenshi) and bring them a present (onenga). Of course, if you cannot stop by personally for some reason, you can send them a new year's greeting card (nengajo), which has, regrettably, more recently been replaced by SMS or e-mail. During this period, children receive small allowances from parents and grandparents (otoshidama) and pine tree decorations (kadomatsu) are placed in front of houses.

Most people also visit a shrine (traditionally three) either right after midnight on New Year's Eve or at least during sanganichi in order to thank the gods for the last year and pray for happiness and health in the new one (hatsu-mode or hatsu-mairi).

Local Festivals

Wakakusa Yamayaki *(4th Saturday of January)*

An annual festival in Nara City, which is primarily famous for the spectacular grass-burning on the hillside of Mount Wakakusa-yama.

It is performed for several reasons: as a ritual for the spirit of the sage that is buried on the mountain, and to avoid bad luck in the new year.

The fire is usually accompanied by fireworks, resulting in a magnificent view of earthly and heavenly fires reaching towards each other.

Sapporo Snow Festival *(early February)*

The biggest festival in all of Hokkaido, which attracts over 2 million visitors annually.

It started in 1950, when local schools organized a snow-themed event with 6 ice statues in Odori Park. Since 1974, several foreign teams from the sister cities of Sapporo (Portland, USA; Munich, Germany; Shenyang, China; Novosibirsk, Russia; Daejeon, South Korea) have been participating as well. If you would like to volunteer, make sure to apply during the previous November!

And, even if you do not wish to participate actively it is more than recommendable to come and stare at the numerous splendid snow and ice sculptures in awe, in the same park where this festival started some 65 years ago.

Yokote Kamakura Festival *(February 15-16)*

Another snow festival held in Akita Prefecture, however unlike the one in Sapporo, the major attractions here are the hundreds of breathtaking igloos called kamakura scattered all around the city.

Each of them hosts a snow altar for the water deity. Several different kinds of delicious rice cakes and rice wine are offered by the local children in exchange for offerings.

Todaiji Omizutori *(March 1st-15th)*

It is also called Shunie and is one of the oldest Buddhist religious services in Japan, with over 1,200 years of history.

It is performed annually at the Todaiji temple in Nara City, by 11 monks (rengyoshu). The name comes from a ceremony, during which the priests descend from the Nigatsu-do hall in order to draw water from a well at the base of the temple late at night between the 12th and the 13th of March.

Another astonishing event during this service is the Otaimatsu, which involves a dozen giant (6-8 m, 40-70 kg) burning torches being lit on the balcony of this hall; the embers falling down allegedly provide the visitors with a safe year.

Kanda Festival *(the weekend closest to May 15 in odd numbered years)*

It is considered to be one of the three largest traditional matsuris in Japan (the other two are Gion Festival in Kyoto and Tenjin Matsuri in Osaka; see below).

The extravagant version is held every other year (odd-numbered years) in mid-May, while the scale is considerably more moderate in the years between. It is certainly an unforgettable sight to witness about 300 Edokkos (people who were born and raised in the Kanda area, which was the city center during the Edo Period) marching through the main streets holding some 100 portable shrines on their shoulders.

If you miss it, or you would like to know more about the history of this festival, make sure to visit the Kanda Myojin Museum (hours: 10:00-16:00, fee: 300 yen for adults).

The shrine itself was originally built in 730 and, even though it has been reconstructed and renovated several times since then, the current buildings are still able to provide you with a dazzling atmosphere. Because of its proximity to Akihabara, it is frequently visited by people, who require divine protection for their digital devices.

You need not miss out either: take home a charm (omamori) to shield your gadgets from malicious forces (1,000 yen).

Asakusa Sanja Festival *(3rd weekend in May)*

The Sanja (literally means "three gods") Festival was born in 1872, when three separate events were merged into one.

It is the annual festival of the Asakusa Shrine, and one of the most representative ones in Japan. During the three days it is organized, as many as 30 groups of men, women and children move around their own community's mikoshis (portable shrines).

There are also floating stages, on which you can watch musicians playing on flutes and drums, as well as dancers moving to their rhythm. Follow them to the shrine, where you will witness the performance of the Binzasara Mai traditional dance.

Kyoto Gion Festival *(July)*

As mentioned above, the Gion Festival in Kyoto is one of the three largest traditional matsuris.

It continues throughout the entire month of July and its name comes from the Gion geisha/entertainment district, although most of the events take place somewhere else. Its history began in 863 during the Heian Period, when a protective festival was held to end a series of disastrous plagues. Currently it is organized together by the Yasaka Shrine and the Yamaboko-cho neighborhood.

The festival reaches its peak during the Yamaboko Junko parades on the 17th and the 24th. The 17th features as many as 32 floats, part of them are yamas depicting scenes from Japanese and Chinese mythology, the rest are hokos that are combinations of portable music halls and museums.

All of them are fairly big and heavy (almost 10 tons). The 24th has 10 umbrella floats and dance performances to offer the onlookers.

Osaka Tenjin Festival *(July 24-25)*

It has been held by the Osaka Tenmangu Shrine since 951. Currently it is one of the largest boat festivals in the world: 3,000 people sail some 100 boats from the Tenma-bashi Bridge upstream, which are lit after dusk as part of the boat processions.

The volunteers are all dressed in 11-13th century imperial-court style clothes and, before embarkation, perform a parade with many portable shrines.

It is also recommended to visit one of the many kagura (Shinto theatrical dance) or bunraku (traditional puppet theatre) stages in the city, but make sure to get back in time to welcome the arrival of the 3,000 people crowd to the shrine, when you can witness the fantastic closing ceremony (around 10pm on the 25th).

Nebuta Festival *(August 2-7)*

This is the festival of giant lanterns depicting historical figures such as samurai warriors, along with birds and other animals. According to one legend, its origins come from a warlord's attempt to wipe out all the Ezo people from Northern Honshu and Hokkaido, during which, much like the story of the Trojan War, he hid his soldiers inside big dolls, and this strategy allowed him to succeed.

In fact, it is said that the Aomori City version represents the departure to the front, and the Hirosaki City version, also called Neputa around there, represents the glorious return.

These two variants have many other different aspects that are definitely worth experiencing.

Akita Kanto Festival *(August 3-6)*

This is another important festival in the Tohoku region besides Nebuta and Sendai Tanabata. Its main focus are the 8 meters long bamboo poles that are decorated with 46 lanterns in the shape of rice plant ears, and weigh approximately 50-60 kilograms.

They are believed to drive away the evil spirits, while people are praying for the good harvest.

Tokushima Awa Odori *(August 12-15)*

A dancing festival that is told to be associated with the celebration of the newly build Tokushima Castle in 1587, during which the feudal lord, Hachisuka Iemasa offered sake to the people and the drunk crowd started to dance with such unsteady movements.

Awa odori can be seen in most of the cities during the Obon season, although none of them compare to the one in Tokushima. Here, besides watching the parade and the stage performances, you are welcome to join the dance at the Odori Hiroba!

Himeji Nada no Kenka Festival *(October 14-15)*

If you think that half-naked people struggling with heavy portable shrines on their shoulders or other structures carrying more half-naked men playing on instruments and dancing was not crazy enough: you should see the kenka matsuri, or the fighting festival, where groups of people clad in different colors deliberately make the shrines collide with each other.

In fact, the bigger the collision, the more the kamis are pleased. The winner's village receives a year of good luck and abudance in harvest.

Jidai Festival *(October 22)*

Its history dates back to 1895, when the construction of Heian Jingu was completed, where two emperors, Kanmu and Komei are enshrined.

 As a matter of fact, October 22 is the day, when Emperor Kanmu moved the capital from Nagaoka-kyo to Kyoto in 794. Its main spectacle is the 2 km long parade, which features an array of about 2,000 people dressed in traditional clothes, starting from the Meiji Period all the way to the time of Emperor Kanmu (Enryaku Era, 782-806).

Abroad

If you cannot visit Japan for some reason, don't panic just yet: there are still plenty of annual festivals abroad that are related to Japanese culture and orginazed by the local nikkei population. Although Brazil and the United States (especially Calfornia State) have the largest Japanese diaspora, you can find quite eye-catching events and celebrations in Germany, France, the United Kingdom, Canada and Malaysia, just to mention a few.

PS: Can I Ask You A Quick Favor?

If you liked the book, please leave a nice review on Amazon! I´d absolutely love to hear your feedback.

Every time I read your reviews... you make me smile. I´d be immensely thankful if you go to Amazon now and write down a quick line sharing with me your experience.

I personally read ALL the reviews there, and I´m thrilled to hear your feedback and honest motivation. It´s what keeps me going, and helps me improve everyday =)

Please go Amazon Now and Drop A quick review sharing your experience !

***

THANKS!

***

Manufactured by Amazon.ca
Bolton, ON